Rosemary Linden

To Rosie and Sam
with much love
from

Brian

December 1994.

One Young Soldier

One Young Soldier

The Memoirs of a Cavalryman

TIM BISHOP

Edited by

BRUCE SHAND

MICHAEL RUSSELL

© Estate of the late Tim Bishop

First published in Great Britain 1993
by Michael Russell (Publishing) Ltd
Wilby Hall, Wilby, Norwich NR16 2JP
Typeset at The Spartan Press Ltd
Lymington, Hampshire
Printed and bound in Great Britain
by Biddles Ltd, Guildford and King's Lynn

ISBN 0 85955 193 8

The publication of this book has been made possible
by the financial help of Tim Bishop's relations and friends
and the 9th/12th Royal Lancers Regimental Association

For Genevieve, Edward and Miranda Attwood,
Tim's grandchildren

ECCENTRIC SOLDIER

Some young soldiers carry, when they're apart,
The portrait of a girl next to the heart.
But one young soldier – does it seem silly? –
Carries the portrait of a thoroughbred filly.
A thoroughbred filly, dainty and trim;
And he wouldn't mind if you laughed at him.

These lines appeared in Punch *in August 1942 and were sent to Tim Bishop by a friend who knew that he always kept a photograph, in his breast pocket, of the wonderful Sun Chariot – owned by the King – which had such a success that year. 'She was a feast for the eyes and had also paid one or two mess bills for me in England.'*

Contents

Editor's Foreword

Somewhere there are – or were – stringent military orders forbidding officers from writing diaries during time of war. Happily for posterity, this regulation has been frequently ignored – not least by Field-Marshal Lord Alanbrooke.

Tim Bishop would have been the last person to have heeded such a prohibition – had he known about it – and he assiduously wrote up his daily impressions throughout his own very active service. These he embodied in a long and absorbing account of his early life, which was still in an unedited and unpublished state at the time of his death.

This I have attempted to reduce to a readable size, discarding, with reluctance, much that was not of military relevance. In this final shape it covers his time in the ranks of the Life Guards, the campaign of May 1940 in France and Belgium and the Desert War. Clayre Bishop, his widow, has been kind enough to trust my literary surgery, though whether I would have received the approval of the writer is problematical – but I hope so.

Apart from his many virtues and talents, Tim was a stickler for style, and this will be apparent in this narrative. His devotion to horses and all that went with them was absolute, allied to an artist's perception of the visual scene, and a writer's sense of atmosphere. Devotion also extended to the 'Arme Blanche', whether horsed or mechanised. It would be hard to better his description of his years in the Household Cavalry, or his evocation of the remarkable – and perhaps to some, idiosyncratic – camaraderie that existed in the 12th Lancers, particularly in North Africa.

I salute his memory, after fifty years of friendship, remembering with nostalgia the times we spent together, often in strange circumstances, but always enlightened by his original and refreshing view of the human situation.

BRUCE SHAND

Maps

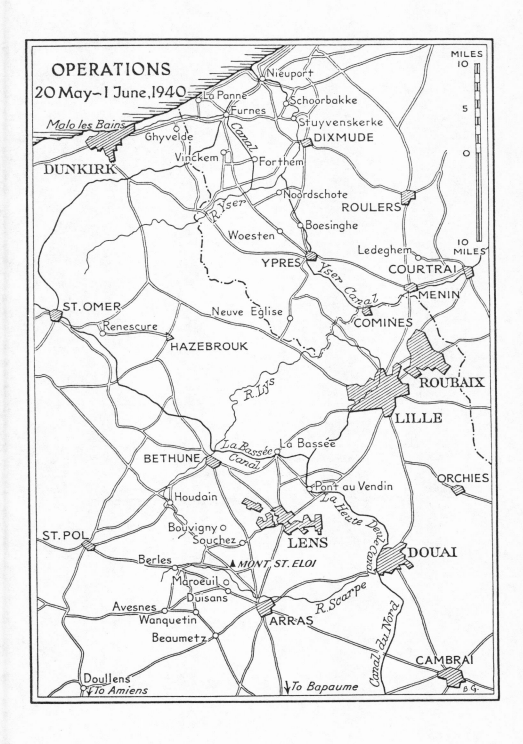

OPERATIONS
20 May–1 June, 1940

MILES
10
5
0
10
MILES

Nieuport
La Panne
Schoorbakke
Furnes
Stuyvenskerke
Malo les Bains
Ghyvelde
DIXMUDE
Vinckem
Fortem
DUNKIRK
Canal
R. Yser
Noordschote
ROULERS
Boesinghe
Woesten
Ledeghem
YPRES
COURTRAI
Yser Canal
MENIN
ST. OMER
Neuve Eglise
COMINES
Renescure
HAZEBROUK
R. Lys
ROUBAIX
LILLE
La Bassée
La Bassée
ORCHIES
Canal
BETHUNE
Houdain
Pont au Vendin
La Haute Deule Canal
Bouvigny
Souchez
LENS
DOUAI
ST. POL
Berles
MONT. ST. ELOI
Maroeuil
Duisans
R. Scarpe
Avesnes
Wanquetin
ARRAS
Beaumetz
CAMBRAI
Canal du Nord
Doullens
To Amiens
To Bapaume
B.G.

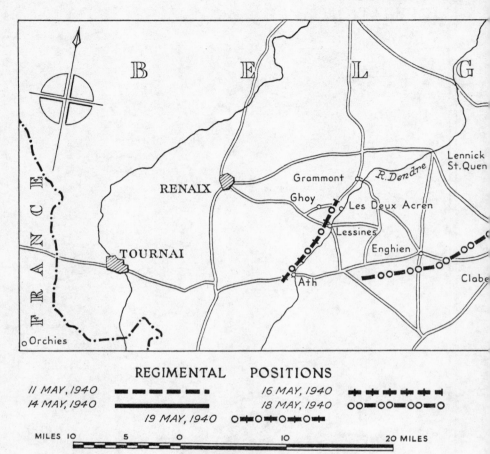

REGIMENTAL   POSITIONS

11 MAY, 1940 ▬ ▬ ▬ ▬   *16 MAY, 1940* ✛▬✛▬✛▬✛

14 MAY, 1940 ▬▬▬▬▬   *18 MAY, 1940* ○○▬○○▬○○▬○

19 MAY, 1940 ○▬○✛○✛○▬

MILES 10 ▬▬▬ 5 ▬▬▬ 0 ▬▬▬▬ 10 ▬▬▬▬ 20 MILES

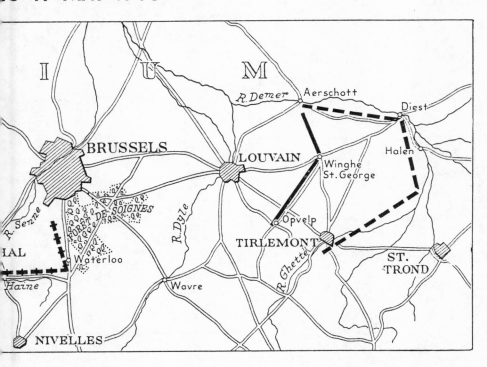

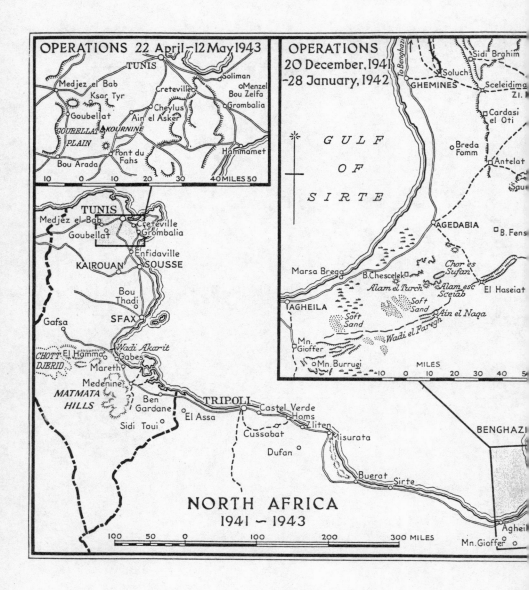

OPERATIONS 22 April – 12 May 1943

TUNIS
Medjez el Bab
Ksar Tyr
Creteville
Soliman
oMenzel
Bou Zelfa
oGrombalia
Cheylus
Goubellat
Ain el Asker
GOUBELLAT KOURNINE
PLAIN
Pont du
Fahs
Hammamet
Bou Arada

10   0   10   20   30   40 MILES 50

**OPERATIONS
20 December, 1941
– 28 January, 1942**

To Benghazi
Sidi Brahim
Soluch
GHEMINES
Sceleidima
Zi.
Cardasi
el Oti
GULF
OF
SIRTE
Breda
Fomm
Antelat
Sau
AGEDABIA
B. Fens
Marsa Brega
B.Chescelek
*Chor es
Sufan*
Alam el Turch
*Alam esc
Sceiab*
El Haseiat
TAGHEILA
*Soft
Sand*
*Soft
Sand*
Ain el Naqa
Mn.
Gioffer
Wadi el Faregh
oMn. Burrugi
MILES
10   0   10   20   30   40   5

TUNIS
Medjez el Bab
Goubellat
Creteville
Grombalia
KAIROUAN
Enfidaville
SOUSSE
Bou
Thadi
SFAX
Gafsa
CHOTT El Hamma
DJERID *Wadi Akarit*
Gabes
Mareth
Medenine
*MATMATA
HILLS*
Ben
Gardane
El Assa
TRIPOLI
Castel Verde
Homs
Sidi Toui
Zliten
Cussabat
Misurata
Dufan
Buerat
Sirte
BENGHAZI

NORTH AFRICA
1941 – 1943

Agheil
Mn. Gioffer

100   50   0   100   200   300 MILES

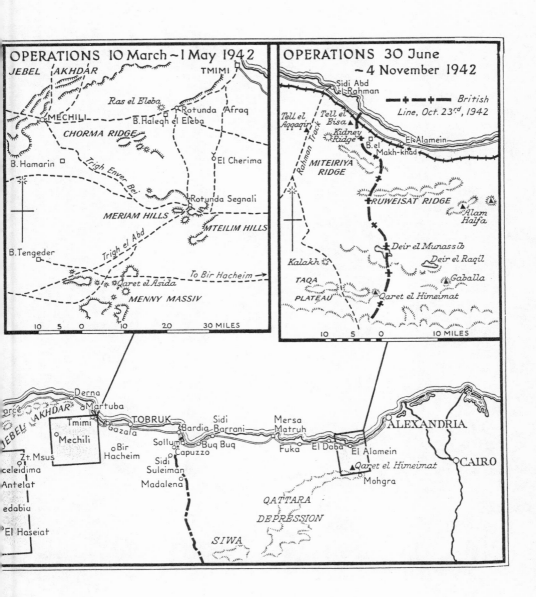

OPERATIONS 10 March ~ 1 May 1942

JEBEL AKHDÁR
TMIMI
Ras el Eleba
Rotunda Afraq
MECHILI
B. Haleqh el Eleba
CHORMA RIDGE
B. Hamarin
El Cherima
Trigh Enver Bei
Rotunda Segnali
MERIAM HILLS
MTEILIM HILLS
B. Tengeder
Trigh el Abd
To Bir Hacheim →
Qaret el Asida
MENNY MASSIV

10 5 0   10   20   30 MILES

OPERATIONS 30 June ~ 4 November 1942

Sidi Abd el-Rahman
Tell el Aqqaqir
Tell el Eisa
━┼━┼━ British Line, Oct. 23rd, 1942
Kidney Ridge
El Alamein
B. el Makh-khad
MITEIRIYA RIDGE
RUWEISAT RIDGE
Alam Halfa
Deir el Munassib
Kalakh
Deir el Raqil
TAQA PLATEAU
Gaballa
Qaret el Himeimat

10 5 0   10 MILES

Derna
Martuba
arce
JEBEL AKHDÁR
Tmimi
Gazala
TOBRUK
Sidi Barrani
Mersa Matruh
ALEXANDRIA
Mechili
Bardia
Bir Hacheim
Sollum
Buq Buq
Fuka
El Daba
El Alamein
Zt. Msus
Capuzzo
Sidi Suleiman
Qaret el Himeimat
CAIRO
celeidima
Madalena
Mohgra
Antelat
edabiu
QATTARA DEPRESSION
El Haseiat
SIWA

I

Enlisting

Tim Bishop was born in 1915, the year which saw the disastrous Gallipoli campaign. His father had commanded, with great gallantry, the 1st Lancashire Fusiliers at W Beach, where his battalion had suffered appalling casualties. After the war Colonel Bishop retired to the New Forest and later on the family lived at Harewood, near Andover. Tim and his sister Molly, to whom he remained very close all his life, had an idyllic childhood. Apart from his passion for horses and hunting he had a profound and knowledgeable love of every aspect of country life.

He said that he never contemplated not being a soldier, and his education started with a somewhat austere private school, to be followed by Stowe, then under the headmastership of the celebrated Roxburgh, who later wrote, presciently, 'An excellent boy out of school, but he can write delightfully and must keep this up.' He was also fortunate with his house master, who had been one of his father's subalterns, and with a sporting clerical member of the staff who let him ride one of his hunters. Stowe lies in the Grafton country – then enjoying the legendary Mastership of Lord Hillingdon – and Tim managed to get an astonishing amount of hunting from school. So much so that difficulties ensued with the School Certificate, a necessary preliminary to the Sandhurst exam.

Rather than go to a crammer of his father's choice he elected to enlist in the ranks . . .

That week I had to go to the dentist in London. The taxi stopped to allow the King's Guard, provided by The Blues, to cross Hyde Park Corner. Lots of black horses clattering into the Park like, I thought, a hunting field moving off from a meet of hounds. What I could see of the moustached faces under the gleaming helmets looked soldierly to me. But I had always preferred the uniform of the Life Guards. (So much for the pull of full dress in recruiting. My father preferred that of The Blues – 'more practical,' he said.) A few days later and feeling slightly crazy, I slipped away to Winchester in a bus and presented myself at the Recruiting Office there, and found it difficult to be taken seriously. I was also surprised and disappointed to learn there was a long waiting list for the regiment of my choice. But they were kind enough to take my particulars and smilingly told me I would be informed when the Household Cavalry was ready for me.

When at last I heard that I was to report to the Life Guards at Windsor, I told my father. For once, he appeared pleased with me. Not only did he drive me there himself – we had lunch on the way – but to my dismay he drove straight past the guard room and swept up to the officers' mess. It was no different from being taken to my preparatory school for the first time and not at all what I expected, intended, or indeed, approved; very far from it.

By the grace of God there was (needless to say in those days) only one officer in the mess; the adjutant, magnificent and moustached, tall and immaculate in his blues and enjoying a post-luncheon cigar. I immediately recognised him as a regular with the Grafton, always most beautifully turned out in scarlet cutaway, leathers and scoured tops. In a way it must have been a unique occasion and he, of course, handled it with tact and charm. But I stood apart, stricken with horrified disapproval and inability to explain that this was 'none of I'.

My father dropped me at the guard room on his way out; from upstairs to downstairs for me with a resounding crash.

2

'Quickest the Best . . . '

The sentry on the front gate made a vivid splash of colour against the background of dull grey and drab fawn buildings of Combermere Barracks.

Entering the guard room was like stepping back into the Napoleonic era. The scene was, considering it was 1934, extraordinarily similar to that reproduced on the dust cover of volume 1 of Lord Anglesey's *History of the British Cavalry*. Corporal of Horse Summers rose to greet me and, with clanking sword and ringing spur, conducted me, politely enough, to a barrack room where awaited four other new recruits. With the exception of the medical officer (a kindly, white-haired colonel) and a fatherly SQMS (who had joined the year I was born), it was the last bit of politeness I was to encounter for many a long day.

Four pleasant-faced, phlegmatic, tall and lanky South Country boys were waiting in the barrack room into which I was ushered. We were probably all in varying degrees nervous. We had just voluntarily put a torch to our civilian boats and this at once brought us closer together. We knew that in order to be a good soldier it was as well to have no ties outside the Army. We also knew that the regiment would, to put it mildly, demand our undivided attention from now on. Most important, we knew and understood that we were 'for it'. So we were prepared to 'take it' or we would not have been there. Otherwise the barrack room in which we were having our first taste of that well-known Army pastime, 'waiting', would surely have appalled us to the extent of our walking back out of the main gate without further ado. There was still time. We had yet to be seen by the Commanding Officer before being 'finally accepted'. But as one of our number had 'got fed up with being a cabinet maker's apprentice', another with 'trudging up and down behind a bloody plough from dawn to dark, day after day, being shat on by seagulls', it seemed unlikely that any of us would turn back.

The room in which we waited was spacious with a high ceiling and situated directly above the stables. A hideous black stove, out in the centre, was guarded all round by a bleak little curb of whitewashed concrete. A dreadful black pipe rose from the stove to disappear through a hole in the ceiling. There was a trestle table and forms. Against the walls, closely aligned, stood diminutive iron bed-steads, without mattresses or blankets, folded to chair size. Three pegs and an empty tin locker served each bed. The floor was of bare boards. As the room was not in use, all was quite remarkably forlorn, the true abomination of desolation. Worse, there was an adjoining 'ablution room' with stone floor, urinal, and cold-water taps – cold water only. Even had one joined out of desperation, as perhaps some boys did, it was a poorish welcome.

But as yet I was only excited with this new adventure. Reading *Beau Geste* had left its mark: I felt quite like one of the Gestes joining the Foreign Legion. (There must be many points in favour of being a romantic.) Also I had the advantage, just there and then, of being born into the Army and brought up with the sole purpose of becoming a soldier. The Army and its ways were not new to me. This obviously helped enormously.

For two hours no one came near us. Normally grey, Windsor Castle, which had looked white in the afternoon sun, turned black as evening and clouds approached. I have since seen the Round Tower turn anything from pink to orange, from violet to pale blue, a great reflector of sunrises, sunsets and moods of the weather. The further side of the square was still patrolled by the sentry, who occasionally took a jingling stroll up and down, the blade of his drawn sword on his right shoulder. As he turned about, reflected lights flashed like heliotropes from various parts of his equipment. Admittedly it did not look very interesting work, but hasten the day, thought I, when I had risen to such heights. It would be at least one rung higher up the ladder.

We were just deciding that we had been forgotten, when a young NCO burst in and took us to 'draw biscuits'. By this time we were feeling in need of something more substantial. But the 'biscuits' turned out to be small mattresses (three laid end to end made one soldier's bed). We also drew blankets and a pillow – canvas, the shape of a suet roll, stuffed tight with horsehair and stone-hard. Lest we dislocate our necks we folded our pullovers, coats or towels for pillows that night. We were then shown the troopers' mess and told to go in and get 'tea'. Somewhat timidly we entered this crowded and noisy room and found ourselves placed on benches at trestle tables with a plate of fried egg and chips. Still clad conspicuously in our civilian suits we were surrounded by cheerfully curious and rowdy soldiers in canvas dungarees that reeked of stables. Their every other word, it seemed to me, was the same four-letter one, even inserted quite often into the middle of ordinary two-syllable words. It was used as a verb, noun or adjective and without inhibition.

The cavalry Reveillé lasts just over a minute. Depending on the condition of the listener or perhaps the weather, or both, it can either be a thrilling sound or, more often, a ghastly one. On our first morning I felt proud to listen to it for it now concerned me personally. But then we recruits were not embroiled in the general hubbub preceding a morning's mounted drill in the Great Park. From the top balcony outside the room, I was to have a bird's-eye view of the squadron to which I had been posted, parading in the early sunshine immediately below. I looked down on a gleaming array of shining cleanliness. Even in khaki the Life Guards were dazzling. The summer coats of the horses shone. Bits, buckles, stirrup-irons, spurs and mess-tins blinked and twinkled. Not only was the steel burnished, buttons, cap-badges and titles winked and flashed. The blue sky was reflected in the polished seats of the saddles (polished seats and surcingles, soaped flaps).

Noticing the steel on some coach harness at Windsor Show forty years later, when riding on a friend's four-in-hand, I asked him, a knowledgeable man, if it was all burnished. 'What', he asked, 'is burnished?' I explained. The coachman intervened. 'It's all chrome nowadays, sir,' he said. Indeed, there were no 'stay-bright' buttons either, in the days of which I write.

Talking of coaches, the regimental coach and two or three others would always be parked beside the officers' stables just before Ascot Week. One would see bays and chestnuts being led to water. It was rather a relief from our interminable blacks and occasional greys. The one time when hardship eased a point, apart from Christmas, was during Ascot Week. In fact, the regiment, when at Windsor, virtually 'closed down'. Special buses were laid on daily for the benefit of those soldiers who wished to attend. Crate after crate of beer would be hoisted aboard and a holiday atmosphere prevailed. I went with them once. We went on the course and though I cannot say I enjoyed it, I can say for what it is worth that I have seen Brown Jack and Steve Donoghue win the Queen Alexandra Stakes over 'Two miles, six furlongs and eighty-five yards', the last of his six victories in that particular race.

As for the scene below me now, I had seen top-class show horses at Olympia, but I had yet to discover how such a bloom could be put on a horse's coat through sheer good regular grooming and feeding. It was a magnificent sight and I began to have the first strong and unpalatable misgivings that I had bitten off more than I could chew. I was number 295010 now with no one to help me but myself. And, clean as they were, some of the men down there were getting hell from their NCOs. One immaculate man, 'standing to his horse' and looking straight to his front, was being informed in tones that could only be described as threatening that he was 'lousy' – which meant in this case that the inside of one of the buckles on his bridle was not quite as bright as the side that showed. Similarly, 'bastard' could even be a term of endearment in those circles. 'Orderly corporal! Put this filthy dirty man in the book!' This meant that the filthy dirty man's name was taken ('You've lost your name,' the orderly corporal would tell him, writing it down) and he would not be allowed to leave barracks until he had appeared before an officer at squadron office. After which it was more than likely that he would still not be allowed to leave barracks.

From where I stood I could also see that the soldiers' navy blue capes were rolled into tight, wrinkle-less 'sausages' and bent into half-moons to fit the rear arches of their saddles to which they were strapped. I saw the snowy pipe-clayed brow-bands, girths and head-ropes. And I took note of the brown leather chinstraps and bandoliers, so highly polished that they also reflected the blue above, and boots that shone as if water were running over them. Could I, unaided, turn myself and my horse out like that? I would almost certainly 'lose my name'. (In fact I never did. I cannot explain this. I must have had an exceptional guardian angel.)

As the squadron mounted and moved off, one of the horses fell with a crash. When a horse's feet go away from under it on tarmac, the crash is instant and violent, it does not go down slowly as if to roll. The soldier, Trooper Borman, had a leg between horse and road, but 'Come on!' yelped an NCO, turning in his saddle as the horse struggled and floundered, 'Get up, you bloody, dozey man!' As the horse got up, its rider had half dismounted, pulling his rifle from its bucket. But his left foot was still in the stirrup and he swung his right leg over, pushed his rifle back in again and rode quickly up into place. About ten seconds covered the incident and I watched with dropped jaw. The files behind hardly had to draw rein. Those in front did not even glance back. Indeed, God help them if they had. But all he got from the NCO was a last warning to 'wake his bloody idle self up!'

It was said that our training was as stringent as that of the Foot Guards with the care of a horse thrown in. But if this harsh discipline – and I think harsh was a fair description – was not surprisingly pretty good misery to live with on occasion, it certainly helped to make the regiment what it was. I have nowhere since come across a comparable camaraderie or ésprit de corps. 'There is no question that from this ruthless discipline the men somehow acquired a feeling of being part of something greater than themselves, which filled them with pride and a sense of enormous superiority to other men.' Not my words, but written about the Foreign Legion. In my opinion it applied equally to the Life Guards of the early thirties.

Regimental pride was shown in so many ways. But I was surprised how angry my room-mates grew concerning things which I would not have thought, before I got to know them, they would have so much as noticed. One such occasion was when the band had played them back from church to the strains of 'Blaze Away'. They said it made them feel like 'boy scouts or Laurel and' (that four letter word again) ' -ing Hardy walking along to *that* stupid' (same word again) ' -ing tune!' And the band was once more in trouble when it turned out onto the square to play them in from manoeuvres. The tune chosen to greet them was 'Little Man, You've Had a Busy Day!' This piece of tongue-in-cheek whimsy on the part of the well-intentioned Director of Music, proved extraordinarily unpopular. As the soldiers came upstairs after turning their horses in, they were spitting with disgust. What a tune to accompany the Right of the Line, no less, back into barracks: as far as I can remember, the words went as follows:

> 'Little man you're crying!
>   I know why you're blue,
> Someone took your kiddy-car away!
>   Got to go to sleep now
> Little man, you've had a busy day!'

I had thought the choice of tune had added a touch of gaiety to proceedings. A little light-heartedness rarely goes amiss. Not so. Their admirable view was all part of this esprit de corps. For there were many who viewed the world outside what is now the Household Division as undisciplined chaos. They probably went through life without changing that view.

Now, from the same balcony, we watched recruits doing dismounted sword drill with parade swords (the Household Cavalryman had two swords, parade and service). This meant that their time for being 'passed out' by the Commanding Officer was drawing near. They would have joined some ten months before us and their drill was good indeed. In that squad was a rosy-cheeked boy called Thompson. He was one day to becoming Riding Master and, as a major, became well-known after the war in Combined Training, a familiar figure at Badminton and, indeed, at most equestrian events.

We newest recruits were now dispersed to separate troops. It was, in those days, the corporal of horse who was most important from our viewpoint, for the troop leader was very rarely seen, a sort of remote deity. I was posted to Corporal of Horse Dedman's troop, and I do not suppose a better cavalry NCO ever rode. A strict disciplinarian and tough as the proverbial old boot, he had a leathery face, a fierce, brushed up moustache and small all-seeing eyes with, thank goodness, an occasional twinkle in them. He tolerated his 'boys' but adored his horses, especially his own, Peggy (B94). (From an old photograph in my possession I do not think she would have been disgraced in the show ring.) Dedman was a martinet, 100% efficient and a great feeder of horses. But the latter came very much first at all times, as indeed they did throughout the regiment. This led to the dry observation of a trooper, on our receiving the order to dismount and lead, when we had only got as far as Datchet en route from Windsor to Knightsbridge: 'On the command "*Carry your horses*",' he muttered, 'give 'em a cant to the shoulder . . .'

So now I was No. 295010 and Trooper Dive from Peasmarsh in Sussex was 295009. I believe his father was head gardener to Lady Maud Warrender and there were to be occasions when I thanked the Lord for the presence of Arthur Thomas Dive. Strong in arm and outlook, he was a help in all sorts of ways. We were later to work alone and harmoniously in a strictly isolated stable at Windsor when a large number of horses came down with strangles.

I was equally fortunate in my 'regimental father', Trooper Anderson. This was the term applied to an old soldier ('Andy' was a veteran of twenty-seven at the time!) into whose charge a raw recruit was given until he had learned the ropes. He treated me with kindness, only occasionally with exasperation and even that tempered by a tolerant humour. He saw to it that I 'got there', which meant getting me on parade in the right place at the right time wearing the right kit. No easy task considering he had his own parades as well. I went out with him once after duty, but his consumption of beer was phenomenal: I do not think he had a limit. One pint was twice as much as I wanted, not from the point of view of getting drunk, but of becoming full. Twenty pints did not seem to worry Andy, spread over 'an evening on the town', from either angle. So our going out together terminated quite naturally and in no way marred our friendship. Far from it. We continued to exchange Christmas cards up to the war. Andy's thigh was broken by a machine-gun bullet in Palestine early on, and this he told me many years later when I was in London to judge hunters at the Royal International Horse Show. I was walking down Park Lane and we instantly recognised each other after thirty years. He was then acting as doorman outside Grosvenor House.

His horse was B68 and known rather unimaginatively as 'Andy', after his owner. He was then an established 'box' horse, which meant he was sufficiently good-looking and well-mannered to be automatically 'turned in' when on King's Guard. I was therefore fortunate to be connected with such a horse, for to be 'turned in' meant a whole night in bed.

When the King's Guard paraded each morning, its members would ride in a circle round the orderly officer (and sometimes the adjutant as well) and the orderly corporal-major who, like judges in the final 'walk round' at the end of a class of show hunters, would 'turn in' the horses of their choice, leaving the others walking around. The riders of the latter would do their sentry-go dismounted. Those who were 'turned in' would be in the boxes. As these were empty from 4 p.m. to 10 a.m., this gave the 'box men' the afore-mentioned restful night. The remainder had to continue sentry duty. So to be connected with a box horse was very important to one's comfort. Andy's B68 was unarguably boxworthy, and when my time came to go on King's, I was occasionally fortunate enough to be allotted B68 through having been Andy's regimental son. Corporal Pickworth's beloved B55 was another good horse. He hated to be teased. Sometimes Corporal Pickworth would point at him and mutter something rude about him. B55 would lay back his ears, bare his teeth and begin moving about in his stall, lifting a hind leg to kick. It was Corporal Pickworth's 'party piece' and perhaps not a very kind one. At all other times he was sweet-tempered. Yet horse and man understood each other perfectly.

The Pinto (B81) was a splendid little character, usually ridden by Trooper MacKenzie. Not all that little, but small for the regiment, he had two white stockings up to and over the knees and his near hind was white to the hock. With their white blazes he and a similarly-marked horse from 'C' Squadron would generally be chosen as the advance points of a Sovereign's Escort and a very well-matched pair they were. Gay and showy, they were the first indication to the waiting crowds of the approach of their Majesties.

Tess (B31) was a sweet, sensible mare. I liked to ride her on watering order (daily exercise) as she did not object to any other horse being led from her back, even one on either side. Trooper Griffin's B35, Trooper Paul's B60 and B61 would have carried the most choosy ladies out hunting, being good-looking, but on the light side for the Household Cavalry. But 'my' Henrietta (B102) was the pick of the bunch – and what a lot all these 'dear, dead horses of long ago' taught me. More of Henrietta anon.

It was also possible – just – to earn a night in bed by being the smartest soldier on barrack guard. If – and it was a big 'if' – you were made 'stick orderly', it meant that instead of joining the roster for sentry duty, you went back to your barrack-room and changed your helmet and plume for a comfortable red and blue forage cap, your sword for a whip, your gauntlets for gloves. You ran a few messages about the place, but you slept in your own bed instead of taking your turn on sentry-go and dossing down in your clothes in the guard room. That was a treat and a half.

Few could compete with the likes of Trooper Rockall (also outside Grosvenor House with Andy after the war) whose large black moustache was the envy of all – King George V decreed, during my time in the regiment, that everyone must grow a moustache. Trooper Shone, too, was well named. He was killed in Palestine early in the war, a tragic waste of a fine man. But, always to my amazement, I was occasionally awarded the stick and it was like a drink of iced beer in the desert.

Now, however, we were but the rawest of recruits, who had not as yet even drawn canvas dungarees in which to work in the stables. Smart uniforms, guards, escorts, 'box'-horses and stick orderlies were a world away and a hard world at that. A Foot Guardsman joined for three years with the colours and it was said that it took those three years to produce him fully trained. We joined for eight (and four on the Reserve) and our recruits' course alone would take a year. In other words we had let ourselves in for twelve years, but, thanks to the war, I was leading a squadron of 12th Royal Lancers within ten years. However, to my disappointment, it was not a gleaming sword but a much-used broom which I was handed (or had hurled at my back) in the half light of the following dawn. Thereafter I spent much time learning by experience the truth within the local jest: 'Join the Army and see the world. Join the Life Guards and sweep it'. But with nearly four hundred horses on the strength, almost non-stop sweeping was essential to keep the place like a new pin. And like a new pin did we keep it.

Several things took a bit of understanding. First, perhaps, the shouting of the NCOs at Reveillé: 'Rise and shine, bed in line etc. etc. The sun is burnin' your bleedin' eye-ball'; and this on a pitch dark and freezing morning in January. Then there was the unofficial but total and dreadful ban on the wearing of pyjamas — that and having to share 'ablution' facilities. In that society it would have been as wrong to wear them as would be a top hat and cut-away coat out cub-hunting. The shirt and underclothes worn during the day were the recognised form of night attire and that was indisputably that. And it is nearly true that you can get used to anything in time. One was usually so tired that it did not matter much anyway. Secondly, the mucking out of stables which followed at 6.30 a.m. using only the bare hands. No stable implements were permitted young soldiers. Nor was so much as a wisp of straw wasted. Bedding that would have been thrown out of a civilian stable was carried, in warm, sticky, ammonia-scented and ton-weight armfuls, to be dumped in the yard (in bad weather under the lean-to sheds) to be spread to dry by 'old' soldiers with forks. It was carried in again, lighter and less pungent, at evening stables. Meanwhile these were swilled out until the last hay-seed was washed away. Breakfast could have been eaten off the floor. And when wisps were made for use at evening stables you made them from this used bedding, never from hay or clean straw. Thirdly, the method employed for removal of grease from new leather spur-straps (the type used for swan-necked spurs and jackboots). They were simply dropped into the urinal and left to lie there for a matter of days. They were then fished out, washed, dried – and, with considerable 'elbow-grease' – at last worked up to a fine polish. Fourthly, the shaving with cold water. One got used to that, too, but the Royal Navy complained bitterly and not really surprisingly when some of its members stayed with us at Windsor for a royal funeral. I was orderly corporal at the time and in the end just had to arrange for hot water from the cook-house to be taken up to them, 'in case', as I explained to my indignant comrades-in-arms, 'we have another Invergordon!'

Fifthly, the food. A slab of yellow, soap-like cheese and one large white and pungent slice of raw onion was quite frequently the last meal of the day – unless, of course, you had sufficient private means to buy your own supper in the canteen later on. Very few had. And a breakfast of bacon smothered in fried onions could surely stymie the hungriest. Sixthly, having to wear ankle boots with nailed soles. In order to get about the stables and yard one adopted a sort of ostler's trot, but at first it was like working on ice. It did make life doubly difficult. The boots of, for instance, Corporal of Horse Wheatley had rubber soles. No doubt he had specific permission. But why did not we all? A quiet, hyper-efficient NCO, his approach was not only sure but silent, keeping the soldiers in his troop on their (steel-plated) toes, wide awake and alert. Seventhly, being constantly taken to task in no uncertain manner for something that could not possibly by any stretch of the imagination be your fault (such as being hauled over the coals because your horse's feet had gone away from under him on the tarmac and given you a crashing fall!)

Eighthly, trying to obey the orders of NCOs who might have been talking Chinese, Russian or Arabic until you got the hang of it. Very early in my Army career I understood the guard commander to tell me to 'nibble the apples for a rhyme in Whaddon Woods'. Rapped out sharply, this strange command had the green listener at a disadvantage, yet to look baffled or to hesitate thereabouts, simply did not do. 'Corporal!' you shouted – and made yourself scarce, finding as quickly as possible a sympathetic interpreter. ('He wants you to nip up the stairs [apples and pears, Cockney rhyming slang] to the canteen for a cheese roll [a rhymer] a bun [a wad] and a packet of woodbine cigarettes.') Like so many things, easy when you know how. The Life Guards had a language of their own and it was as well to learn it with all dispatch. For instance, the order to 'Get a rift on that chain'. To polish your horse's collar-chain you first dropped it in the gutter of your horse's stall and rubbed it about with your foot. You then picked it up, washed and dried it by rubbing it vigorously on the top of an unopened bale of straw. When it was dry, you put it into a sack or stable rubber which you had previously filled with shredded paper or clean straw. You then shook and tossed the sack until you had got a rift on the chain, a rift meaning, I suppose, the required sparkle.

Again, if someone was described as 'ticking' or 'bobbery' it meant that he was angry. And if an NCO warned you that you would be 'First relief chicks', he meant that your sentry duty would be carried out under the arches either side of the stables' entrance into the Horse Guards. This was officially known as 'Over the Arms', but unofficially as 'The Chicken Run' and was where the least smart members of the guard were posted. Initially, like so much else, it all called desperately for interpretation. A rifle was a 'bandook', 'browned off' was fed up, 'gippo' was gravy and 'duff' was pudding. The fair sex were 'cows'.

'Where is your Tom Clark?' was another question that could leave the raw recruit silent. A Tom Clark was a stable rubber dipped into a bucket of water and then wrung out as dry as possible. Put to immediate use it was a wonderful thing with which to lay the dust on the surface of a horse's coat just before showing him out to an NCO after grooming.

But it did seem to me as time went by that things were made as arduous and uncomfortable as was humanly, or inhumanely, possible. The times for recruits' parades were so arranged that it was impossible, for instance, to be dismissed from one riding school, turn in your horse, change your clothes and present yourself punctually and properly turned out for the next – perhaps the square (meaning drill with or without swords or rifles) unless, that is, you went without breakfast. By missing this meal, however, we managed to do it and thereby, I suppose, learned over and over again that it is possible to achieve the impossible. A recruit received much the same treatment as does a tennis ball during a prolonged rally. The Inspector-General of Cavalry said of recruits in the 1890s that they 'hardly had time to eat their dinners'. Forty years later, neither had we.

Anyway, I never suffered such discomfort or was so rushed, even during six years of war. Perhaps anyone bothering to read this might think 'What did the fool expect?' Well, the fool expected what he got, though there is a difference between what you expect and the actual experiencing of it. But the fool was comforted in the knowledge, even then, that the happiest regiments are the best disciplined.

But to this day I still consider it pretty mean of the War Department of those times to expect soldiers, who were daily supposed to represent all that was smartest in the British Army and whom tourists from all over the world travelled miles to see, to wash *and shave* in cold water. However, one cannot deny that the general policy was one that worked. If you have a lot of young men who, because they are young men, are fairly pleased with themselves, you have to give them 'a bit of stick' or discipline suffers. For pleased with ourselves we must have been to have wanted to don a uniform that was going to take so much wearing and looking after (we had, for a start, got two different cap badges, let alone swords), and of riding a horse that also had to be looked after and never left because, always stabled, it was incapable of looking after itself. 'Il faut souffrir pour être bel?' Suffer we assuredly did. Hell was most generously dispensed.

Now we were to be 'finally accepted'. Before this we had had a medical examination. The medical officer was a charming, white-haired colonel who surprised me very much by urging me when I was left alone with him 'not to go through with this'. Amazingly, he was the exact equivalent of the charming French colonel who tried to dissuade John Geste from joining the Legion. I appreciated his advice now as I did then, perhaps even more, but I am thankful to say that his kind (and wise) words went unheeded. He was of course absolutely right. In my opinion, at an impressionable age, service in the ranks is not beneficial, whatever some clowns (who never had to do it) might, or still do, preach. Future officers should not start in the ranks. Nothing could ever convince me that it is either right or 'a good thing'. The M.O. had a son at Eton and his words had been heartfelt. But, speaking for myself, and only for myself, if I could get my commission this way instead of swotting at some crammers, then nothing on earth could have turned me from my purpose.

A year later when he had to lecture everyone with under three years' service on the perils of VD, the same M.O. motioned me to wait behind when the assembly was dismissed. He then actually apologised, did this great gentleman, for not noticing that I was present until too late. I suppose he thought I might feel degraded. I was already (more or less, never totally) hardened to all the physical indignities. But, my goodness, I appreciated his kindness. Later again, when once more I was medically inspected before my interview for a place at Sandhurst, he offered me a ticket for a Rugby International at Twickenham! He was a lieutenant-colonel, I an acting lance-corporal. And in a regiment where, I would say, the gulf between was as wide as you would find it. I had voluntarily joined the Great Unprivileged and it is not a happy experience. The M.O.'s understanding and decency towards me could have gone no further and I shall always be grateful.

Fortunately I was — and probably too often have been — swayed by glamour. Through all the hardships of the next few years, glamour, often a shade elusive, was nearly always somewhere at hand. The wedding escort for Prince George and Princess Marina was an example, particularly the afternoon party which accompanied them to the station en route for their honeymoon. It clattered back into Hyde Park Barracks after dark in the foggy wet of that November evening. Yelling of orders, scarlet cloaks, clanking scabbards and steaming horses in the lamplight . . . But for the continuous background roar of London's traffic we might have been back in the seventeenth century.

Again, there was the daily pageantry of the King's Guard riding out and the Old Guard coming in, both to the strangely monotonous yet grand tones of the Royal Salute, suddenly amplified as the trumpeter rode under the archway. To my (entirely inexpert) ear the same note occurs very approximately forty-four times in a call of about fifty-five notes in all. Different trumpeters had their own way of sounding calls – after a while one could tell which trumpeter was sounding. To ride out in May into the fresh young greenery of Hyde Park, with its clouds of blossom and banks of tulips, held a different glamour. The Park took on a sort of lively expectance, a zest in its promise of summer and the Season. Astride a horse, surrounded by finery and with the prospect of an afternoon's racing at Windsor or Hurst Park, I felt seduced by it. In June came the Trooping, with the regiment trotting past the King, its Colonel-in-Chief, to the carefree lift of the 'Keel Row'. The sun struck heliotrope flashes from cuirass and helmet as, all a-glitter, we wheeled round knee to knee, the Admiralty on our right, the ruler-straight ranks of the Foot Guards forming a scarlet wall on our left.

Twenty trumpeters sounding 'Stables' under the clock at Knightsbridge at 11 a.m. added another touch of glamour, so I thought. And every night Last Post floating up from the darkness below had the power to stop me in my tracks. At such times I would think 'Who would be a civilian?' Now that I am one, I still do, but the saying 'Once a Life Guard, always a Life Guard' is quite a comfort.

Even the rough riders (so called though they were anything but) out in the Row on the young horses destined for duty with the regiment, had, though they would have been most surprised to hear it, a certain glamour. These were the soldiers I envied, the Riding School staff. They were men apart, in Hessian boots (as opposed to puttees) and carrying long polo whips instead of the regimental pattern. They did not have to 'muck out', their horses were turned out for them and taken off their hands when they dismounted, and they did no guards. To dig, one might say, they were ashamed, though they occasionally had to loosen the tan round the school's perimeter. Their job was to take the green horses and turn them into trained troop horses. And in charge of them was Squadron-Corporal-Major Wyer, a cavalryman of the old school from the top of his red, blue and gold cap down to his burnished spurs.

I admired Corporal-Major Wyer as I have admired few other men. He was hardness personified. If he rode up beside you in the school, your horse might nearly rub your leg off against the wall. If he was displeased, which appeared to be most of the time, he would hold the ride and have the recruits mounting and dismounting without stirrups (he favoured 'up the offside, down the near') until their faces resembled wet Dutch cheeses. (We also did physical training under the correct, but far less severe, Corporal-Major Woods, and we drilled (and drilled) under the comparatively kind, if rugged, Corporal of Horse Farmer and the impeccable Corporal Whitfield.) But it was the pitiless hands of Corporal-Major Wyer that moulded young troopers into the right shape (his gentle hands he reserved for young horses), so that when the regiment galloped past Kind Edward VIII in Windsor Great Park in 1936 His Majesty was reported to have remarked that the lines of the galloping half-squadrons were 'as inflexibly straight as blocks of wood'. Watching the newsreels the same evening they looked to be just that. The pace was a gallop, the soldiers in full review order (the officers wearing frock coats and forage caps by order of the King, because he himself was thus attired) and, because swords were drawn, the reins were held in the left hand only. I of course thought it all superb. It was – and the credit largely Wyer's. His Majesty even noticed that the farrier-major's buttons on that occasion were 2nd Life Guards!

At the parade's conclusion, we were played back to barracks down the sun-flooded Long Walk to the strains of 'Colonel Bogey'. This tune had, as every soldier knows, a special significance which at first made it seem to me unsuitable. But with the King riding at our head it soon began, with its second part, to sound grander than all the symphonies. An aura of splendour surrounded one, from the glossy black quarters of the horses in front to the gilt and silver of royal cyphers emblazoned here, there and everywhere around. Immediately after such parades just about everything else seemed boringly ordinary.

But that was in 1936, two long years ahead. To fit us for such occasions, Wyer's training had been hard, but he never told anybody to do anything he could not do (better) himself. Nowadays, stools are provided from which soldiers in Queen's Guard Order may more easily mount their horses. Why not? Very sensible. But I think I know what SCM Wyer would have thought of them. He would have personally kicked them away from under our feet. In those days he would.

Soon after I joined, the regiment moved to Pirbright where we were under canvas, the horses in 'lines'. I shared a bell tent with four other soldiers. There was never a cross word and I do not think I had ever laughed so much.

Towards the end of our time there, a handy horse trial was held. Wyer competed, which I considered a courageous thing to do. As with many professionals, there were those who would have dearly loved to see him beaten. But of course he won easily. He went fast and, where possible, took obstacles at an angle that could have invited refusals in other men's hands. This was in the days before the British Show Jumping fraternity adopted the Continental style of getting a move on and competitions 'against the clock'. The British show-jumping fraternity were few and mostly from Weedon. Perhaps, by today's standards, they were over-careful to 'see their stride'? But Wyer was ahead of his time.

Grip and balance he taught us. For a soldier expected to do his fighting on horseback, grip was highly important. 'Look!' he would yelp and, to be sure, we were looking all right. There he was, knees higher above the saddle than Lester Piggott's, arms outstretched and gripping with his calves. 'If I can do it, so can you!' The fact that he wore boots while we wore puttees was not lost upon us, but we had to try.

'You're like a lot of fancy women!' he cried and within seconds had us going over the whole line of horses without using stirrups, up the off side and down the near and straight on to the next horse until we had been over every horse in the ride. 'Quickest the best!' accompanied his every order. As, puce in the face, panting and gasping, we settled ourselves in our own saddles once more, he would bark 'You idle crew! *Now* try!' But of course by then, as well he knew, we were even less capable.

To start with, however, our ride was taken by a hard-as-nails Scottish corporal. Compared with the comparative kindness designed to encourage the learners of today, our instructor just stared at us in horrified disbelief. Then: 'So *you*', and we jumped at the suddenness of his shout, '*you* think you are going to be Life Guards?' He turned his horse and circled us at a collected trot, very nicely done. Then he faced us once more. I liked him when I became a corporal myself, but now his eyes were not friendly. 'It is my view', he said, 'that given luck *none* of you will survive.' He rode another circle, fist on thigh, before addressing us in a more quietly reasonable tone. 'For a mon like me who loves his harses,' he explained, 'it *hurts* to see people like *you* having the dammed impairt'nance to try and set on their backs.' (Thanks very much!) But looking back, his was not an easy task. One of us was, as I have said, a cabinet-maker from, I think, Portsmouth. Another had been a policeman on the beat who, on a horse, appeared at first to be made of wood. A third had come all the way from South Africa to join what he termed the 'World's Most Famous Regiment', and was to be disappointed in the life it offered at Windsor. He had ridden all his life, but not exactly in the style required here.

He almost at once began 'going absent'. He was a nice man, but if he wanted to do something else, he just went and did it – without asking leave – and always seemed to be in the guard room. Another recruit, son of a well-to-do grocer, had probably fancied the idea of riding through London with the King and Queen. He got his father to buy him out within the fortnight. (It cost £30 then and the others had not got thirty *shillings* even had they wanted to go.)

I have never been able to understand why the man who is naturally kind, good-natured and thoughtful for others (he does exist) hardly ever commands respect (the 'easy' schoolmaster, for example). Wyer was none of these things, was rarely off a horse and shared his room over the Park entrance with his Alsatian dog. But men respected him. When I remember the Life Guards, I remember Frankie Wyer, wire indeed and whipcord too. When one got up in the morning, he could be seen trotting round the School awaiting his first ride to parade. Late in the evening he was still at it, instructing perhaps a class of Yeomanry (Inns of Court).

As for dismounted sword drill in an icy Knightsbridge alleyway on a pitch-dark winter's morning, it was a kill-or-cure operation. If our riding instruction was gruelling, dismounted sword drill was equally so in a different sort of way. 'Cavalry men to your right front . . . ENGAGE!' There we stood, our knees bent, our feet the width of a horse apart, our left hands clutching our middles as if holding the reins, our drawn swords as extension of our right forearms, straight, we hoped, from elbow to sword point.

'POINT!' At this we drove our swords into the imaginary guts of the imaginary enemy cavalryman. And in that position we were kept, our posteriors now well stuck out, our right arms fully extended, this time straight from shoulder to sword point. Corporal-Major Wyer might then take a stroll up the bank, ostensibly to check his watch by the guard room clock. Meanwhile our swords begin to weigh doubly heavy, trebly . . . Our fingers were painful from the frost, our muscles beginning to cry out so that swords started to tremble like reeds in a breeze. Stifled gasps would escape the weaker brethren.

We were then 'a miserable shower' (correct) 'of nancies' (incorrect) and we would be sent off to double to the Riding School and back, last home to do it again or 'lose his name'. At least this warmed us up. But to be 'put in the book', thus 'losing our name' to its threatening pages, was our local and permanent Sword of Damocles. Even for the more saintly, trouble waited impatiently round every corner. A London fog could dull the cleanest brass while we waited out in the yard to be inspected. The brightest steel could give the impression of having a speck of dust if inspected in sunlight. Watches can suddenly go slow, alarms fail to go off. Rifle barrels can contain a spot of rust especially if the inspecting NCO has a hangover. And if a horse got a 'tread', the soldier who had been riding the horse immediately behind went automatically into the cells until an officer was available to deal with such careless horsemanship. On top of which, one NCO (later and suitably detached for duty at Aldershot's dreaded 'Glass House') had that unattractive habit of taking one's rifle with which to demonstrate to the squad. The slight feeling of superiority at having one's own rifle chosen died a nasty death when it was suddenly hurled back without warning in mid-sentence. The clumsy Lee-Enfield would be difficult enough to catch at any time, let alone when hurled at cold and unsuspecting hands. To drop a rifle was a heinous offence. As luck would have it, I never did. But we were given every chance and, in the process, lost the odd bit of skin off our fingers.

A recruit's day was planned so that it was impossible for him to sit down unless it was to clean kit or snatch a hurried meal. Dismissed from the ride, we had our beds to make, not for a cosy night's rest, but for the pitiless inspection with everything folded as per regulations, even the iron beds into chair size. The blankets had name-tapes sewn on and folded; these tapes had to be in a ruler-straight line. Blankets were not always strictly rectangular so that the more carefully folded, the less likely were the corners all to meet exactly. We had the room – large enough to accommodate thirty or so beds – to clean every day and to scrub regularly. Buckets of cold water were thrown down followed by handfuls of soft soap. Stable brooms, with bristles upside down, were then employed to scrub. More buckets were followed by 'squeegees' (a rubber bar replacing the bristle) and the dirty water was swilled out of the barrack-room doors and down the iron staircases to the drains in the yard below. Clean water was then used with squeegees following. Those in first-floor rooms over the stables did well to have a care how they descended to the yard if the top-floor rooms were 'on room scrubbing' especially if they were 'going on King's'. 'Eyes down!' was ever the cry, though 'up' would surely have made more sense? For a filthy Niagara could come splashing mercilessly to earth any moment through the myriad iron steps and railings overhead. It was the epitome of discomfort, but made for admirable cleanliness. For one thing, soldiers returning from London outings were all too often sick.

After room-scrubbing, leaving but little time to scrape the fried onions away from our breakfast bacon, there was drill. It seemed that the lynx-eyed NCO who inspected us always hated us. It was probably the same loyal outlook that our Scottish instructor had displayed in the Riding School – 'How dare you think *you* can be Life Guards?'

When all that was over, it was musketry. This was comparatively restful under the tutelage of Corporal of Horse Fitzwater, a familiar figure on retirement in the unsaddling enclosure at Ascot, immaculate in green coat and top hat with gold band. As an instructor of musketry his eyes, like his brilliantly burnished buttons, had a permanent twinkle, luckily for us. 'Lying load!' he would shout and, when we were all settled on our stomachs, 'Blissful! Ain't it?' Well, yes, it was. Out in the Park in the mornings, '*Lovely*! Isn't she?' he would say as an especially pretty typist tapped by on high heels. 'Every morning at the same time! Wonder where she works? PAY ATTENTION!'

He kept order as well as any other NCO, nor was discipline in any way impaired during a short break at rifle instruction one day in the indoor range at Windsor. He had just lit a cigarette when he noticed a sparrow on a rafter down the far end of the building. He picked up a rifle and shot it. Thirty seconds later an irate officer who had been in the Riding School field burst in through the main door. The Corporal of Horse squeezed out the cigarette with one hand behind his back saying that a 'rest' had slipped sideways as he fired at a target . . . He got away with it and in no way lost our respect.

Eventually the time arrived when we were allowed out of barracks *à cheval*. Before sallying forth, however, we were warned that anyone who blew his nose or 'grinned at a fancy woman' (*sic*) would be for the high jump. This was about the time that the King had decreed that the Household Cavalry should all wear moustaches – in some blond cases without much effect. 'And I'll have none of your Gaumont-British efforts either,' yelped the Corporal-Major, '*moustaches* I said. Proper ones!'

After 'dinner' it was more drill and then school. The schoolmaster was Corporal of Horse Roberts and, fortunately for us, another NCO with a sense of fun. Coming straight from the teachings of such as J. F. Roxburgh, I also found it fairly hilarious, with my fellow pupils smoking cigarettes and giving unusual answers to questions – e.g. 'What is the origin of the flashcord, Smith?' 'It carried the key of the old man's padded cell, Corporal.' (The red flashcord on the white pouch belt originally carried the keys of the royal coach.) I took my Certificates of Education, starting by having to read aloud to an officer. ('Oh God! Stop! Stop!' cried Gerry Fuller.) But at least school was another chance to sit down.

The end of the day was spent in doing evening stables and cleaning up for the morrow. All too quickly dawn would find us once again under the merciless eye of SCM Wyer. His teaching may have been hard, but he was fair after his fashion and had no favourites. Months later, when I was on NCO's training at Windsor, he suddenly barked: 'What's the matter, Bishop? You're riding DAMN BAD!' My father had asked me to lunch at The Rag and I had been wondering, as we trotted round, which would be less awful, the electric train to Waterloo and the Underground, or a Green Line bus from the barrack gate to Hyde Park Corner. No one except the officers then had cars. I had been miles away and came to with a jolt. His thinly-veiled contempt for the officer who was supposed to be running the Musical Ride (for which we were rehearsing under Wyer and no one else) was positively embarrassing – and both surprising and very unusual in those quarters. These rehearsals had started dismounted, in the Riding School, and some of the participants aping horses (provided the SCM had left the building for a moment) were extremely funny. At least, they were funny to those who knew horses.

As autumn came, bringing its annual exchange of quarters with the Blues, we recruits willingly embarked on our new life in an attitude of 'Take what comes. It's what you make it.' That year the Blues came to Windsor. The Life Guards rode to London.

3
Dutyman

The exchange of quarters was an annual affair. Every October the Life Guards exchanged homes with the Royal Horse Guards (Blue). The two regiments passed each other on the Great West Road. So I was surprised and delighted when, instead of having to travel in the back of a 3-ton lorry with the other recruits, I was told that I would be riding to London with the regiment. There had, of course, to be a catch. In this case it was The Chink, the horse I was detailed to ride to Hyde Park Barracks, S.W.1. He was an old horse, but still shapely enough for duty, whose age-sunken eyes had earned him his name. Dear Chink. I soon discovered that he could not, or rather would not, keep up at a walk, so had to jog to maintain the correct interval. By the time we had reached Datchet, I saw why I had been so privileged to ride to Knightsbridge. If it was bad enough for me to keep breaking into a jog, how much worse for the normally level-tempered files behind. So I jogged gently from Datchet to Knightsbridge. I should have realised sooner that treats were not, as a general rule, handed out in the Life Guards. There were, however, compensations.

The fine London evenings, for example. After dark and duty one felt that the roseate glow must almost have been visible from Dublin to Denmark. Even now, as the jet banks for its run into Heathrow, I find it exciting to see the lights of London spread out below like a carpet of spilled jewellery. One always felt the charged atmosphere of autumnal London. And I preferred Knightsbridge to Windsor. Country-bred and country-loving as I was, there was always an aura of excitement in the constant roar of traffic, the lights of Sovrani's and the Knightsbridge Grill just across the street, the feeling of being at the hub of the universe. Much good it did us recruits. Apart from the fact that we were not actually locked in at night, and there were no bars on the windows, we might have been in prison. We even referred to Civvy Street as 'Outside'. On at least one occasion when we were outside, we were not allowed in. We had been ordered to watch the regiment play football and the orderly corporal howled that 'anyone seen slipping back into barracks before the end of the match will go straight inside' (inside, on this occasion, referring to the cells). That was one match I watched to the bitter end. Orderly corporals meant what they said.

As for going *out*, we could do so after evening stables until 11.59 p.m. provided we were not on night guard, that everything was clean for the next day and that we had a pass signed by an officer. One of the lures to passing out and becoming a dutyman (or trained soldier) was that we would then have earned a permanent pass, which would allow us out all night, every night, in plain clothes when not on guard. Queen Victoria had endowed the Life Guards with this privilege. Otherwise an order had been very recently issued that we must not even *look* out of the windows on the Park side. Was someone afraid we would blow kisses to the pram-pushing nursemaids who gathered to watch the King's Guard ride out, or the waitresses riding hirelings in the Row? To make matters worse, the forbidden windows were always wide open till evening. In fact after room-scrubbing, if there was a severe frost, the room floors could be slippery. To those who had to spend their time in these rooms and who had nowhere else to go when the NAAFI was closed or the library locked, one might have thought the stoves would have come in useful. But these miracles of black lead, burnished metal and whitewash were only lit *in extremis* by those who had to keep them that way. Furthermore winter was deemed to begin on a certain date, just as the lights were officially switched on from the mains at a given time and not a moment before. Only once was there an open show of discontent, and that was when a London pea-souper fog suddenly turned everything pitch dark at half three in the afternoon. A lot of soldiers were trying to clean up for King's or barrack guard and they could not see. A low growl eventually rose rumbling from the rooms, a dangerous sound because it was invective reinforced by common sense. The lights came on and an industrious quiet returned to Hyde Park Barracks.

There was a serious 'flu epidemic while we were in London. Gargling parades at Reveillé were instituted. We dressed by the right in the early dark and in canvas-clad ranks, mugs in the right hand, gargled and spat by numbers into the gutter that divided square from stable-block. No one could say we were not being trained to put up with the discomforts of war.

The training stood us in good stead once in 1935 when Stoney Castle Camp at Pirbright became flooded out. The regiment went there to fire on the rifle ranges. Otherwise it was a case of riding exercise bareback, grazing the horses and looking after them in open air lines. It was a change of scene and as near relaxation as we were likely to get. But now as the rain pelted down, muddy water in the horselines rose above the shackles and their pegs, while inside our bell tents, it came over the tops of our ankleboots. There were no floorboards.

If there was a lot of cursing, there was little more than usual. Rather was it an occasion for increased jocularity. I sat on the top blanket of my neatly folded bedding (the bottom two were under water) laughing at the observations of my companions. It must have been the possible loss of condition of the horses or the fear of cracked heels that decided the issue. We were, to our amazement, ordered back immediately to London. And we rode there in the day, off-saddling but once to water beside the Thames at Staines.

While on the subject of discomfort by water, I think scrubbing the stable implements while doing stable guard on a Sunday morning in mid-winter must take the palm. I was told to get on with it in an east wind which fairly whistled in from the alleyways beneath Albert Mansions. After breaking the ice, which had already re-formed after early watering, I worked all morning up to the elbows in these troughs. One wore shirtsleeves because to have kept on a 'woollie' would have brought instant criticism from somewhere on high like a ton of bricks. One put everything except the wheelbarrows in to soak. Then one scrubbed forks, brooms, shovels, buckets and feed-tins (there were a lot of these) until one was sure they would dry spotless. Then one scrubbed and swilled the barrows. Obviously when one had done all that, one had to leave the troughs scrubbed white and refilled to their brims with crystal-clear water. I would run into the stables about once every five minutes to push my arms under the rugs of some horse, the best of natural radiators.

The class of recruits to which I belonged was distinguished in having a newly-joined young officer, who rode, drilled and did P. T. with us. The best compliment I can pay him is that, in the Riding School, not one of us objected (in our hearts, I mean, for we certainly would not have done so aloud!) when *he* was allowed to sit still while *we* were being punished, mounting and dismounting without stirrups, running from horse to horse etc. That he was physically incapable of such acrobatics was taken for granted, though I have to confess that the order: 'Sit still the officers! Remainder down the near end and up the off, three times, DOUBLE!' did not seem entirely fair, even in 1934. Also, when his turn came to drill the squad and he had us marching full tilt for the horses' bedding drying in the yard, we stepped shorter and shorter till we were nearly marking time to give him a chance to remember on which foot to give the 'about turn'. Possibly, of course, also to save our shining boots from the manure. But if he chose the wrong foot we, prepared for the eventuality, put in a short one and turned together. We never let him down.

I have said that there were no treats, but in fact, when we had been finally 'passed off' by the Commanding Officer, this young officer stood us all an evening at the theatre by way of celebration. He has since been Joint-Master

of a famous pack of foxhounds in the Shires, like his father before him. He
died, alas, in 1976.

One reason why this favouring of the officers was accepted without
question or rankle was the general view that as they were competent or lucky
enough to have got a commission in such a regiment, then they were indeed
privileged persons which we, as yet, most certainly were not, nor deserved to
be. But at least it gave us an urge to gain promotion. A popular true story – I
was there – was of an incident on the Pirbright ranges when snap-shooting
was about to start.

Officer i/c firing point: 'Don't fire the first exposure!' (This meant that
when the targets rose into view for the first time, it was only to show how long
they would stay in view each time before dropping back out of sight.) But –

'Bang!' (from just one rifle).

Officer i/c firing point: 'Who's that bloody fool?'

NCO i/c firing point: 'Captain The Lord . . . , sir!'

Officer i/c firing point: 'As you were the "bloody fool". Carry on firing!'

Three other subalterns arrived a little later on. One had been in Chandos
with me at Stowe. They were all well liked. They were very fair amateur
steeplechase jockeys for one thing, as was a fourth who, later again,
transferred to us from a line cavalry regiment which had been ordered to
India. He rode in even more races than the others (no doubt his reason for the
transfer) but he was a different, more 'varminty' type. Soon after his arrival he
hobbled on to the square to inspect the King's Guard accompanied by a
couple of greyhounds, a whippet and a Jack Russell. But after one of the
whippets had lifted its leg against the mirror-like jackboots of the right
marker, the practice was discontinued. After which it also became noticeable
how his initial 'mateyness' also ceased with an unattractive abruptness. He
became aloof, like the others, but self-consciously so. In the case of the rest
they always had been, a state of affairs both understood and approved.
Someone must have told him 'We don't do that there here.'

Another subaltern owned a pet raccoon. On one enjoyable occasion he was
seen to be talking to a towering and fierce-looking corporal-major. The latter
was, of course, standing strictly to attention in spite of the raccoon clinging
half way up his thigh. The subaltern appeared not to notice.

I was fortunate in my own troop leader, who was another officer I had
often seen hunting with the Grafton. He actually spoke to me once and I
reminded him of this over forty years later between intervals of walking up
grouse on one of the loveliest of August days. As we stood knee-deep in
heather, the pollen from which was hampering the dogs' search for a dead
bird, 'In those days', he told me, 'the Commanding Officer ran the regiment

through his adjutant, his warrant officers and NCOs. It was considered a futile waste of time for anyone else to put in an apearance!' The C.O. preferred his officers to 'busy themselves with hunting, race-riding and polo rather than have them hanging about in Knightsbridge.'

Funnily enough, when a certain young officer, as orderly officer of the day, once actually appeared in his frock coat in the winter darkness of Reveillé stables, it temporarily lost him the respect of the soldiers to a man. They preferred the raccoon's owner (a viscount) who was fairly regularly driven back into barracks at Windsor by his servant about 5 a.m., pale as death and asleep in white tie and tails, but on his horse at the head of his troop, ready for troop training in the Great Park by 9 a.m.

On the other hand, the adjutant was expected by these same soldiers to be exactly what indeed he was, keen, ultra-smart, a model of elegance and a good soldier. He was just and suitably intimidating in the distant manner then adopted. When on 2 p.m. recruits' parade on any weekday we saw that it was he and not the orderly officer who was bearing down on us, there was an almost audible groan. He was to become my squadron leader and, in time, Commanding Officer of the regiment. But his eye for detail missed nothing and he had no pity if, for example, gold braid looked worn or white gloves needed renewing. For men drawing ten shillings a week, and who had to pay for extra cleaning materials such as Cherry Blossom polish, yellow dusters etc., having to buy new white gloves or gold braid was taxing, to say the least of it. But obviously no hint of shabbiness could be tolerated.

One day there was a small kit inspection. Each man 'stood to his bed' on which lay, faultlessly aligned and all correct, his personal kit. But not 'all correct' was the kit of the soldier opposite me. He had mislaid a pair of white gloves . . . As the squadron leader entered the room and we crashed to attention, he laid his whip and gloves on the trestle table before starting his inspection. The trooper bided his time before, to my absolute horror, snatching up these sacred gloves, he folded them with one deft movement and flicked them onto his kit. On his return journey, the squadron leader, followed closely by the squadron corporal-major, squadron quarter master corporal, squadron orderly corporal and room corporal – all with eagle eyes and note-books at the ready – checked each kit and found all well. As the shining procession moved on, the trooper, judging his moment to perfection, flipped the gloves back onto the table. Presumably he was able to borrow a pair until the next inspection. In the meantime, he would certainly be able to buy himself an extra glass of beer or two. But I think his daring took a year off my life.

When in years to come I was introduced to this squadron leader at a dinner, I did not tell him of this. But his remembering of me after nearly half a century greatly surprised my host of the evening, who said as much.

'You must remember', came the gentle explanation, 'that we were then a very select party.' Which reminds me of another of my Life Guard officers who was kind enough to put me up that I might judge the Ridden Hunter Classes at the South of England Show from a comfortable base rather than from a hotel. His ex-soldier-servant was still with him. Without knowing it, we had been troopers at the same time but, as officer's servant and dutyman, our paths had never crossed. I said something to the effect that it was extraordinary how many characters and incidents one could still clearly remember. He said: 'I think sir, it is because it was such a *special* regiment.'

There was another captain, a mere baronet, whom we all liked. When he came swaggering into the yard after coming off King's, still in his white leathers and jackboots, but with his scarlet tunic and cuirasses changed for a blue patrol tunic, his helmet and plume for a red, blue and gold forage cap, his smartness was an example to all. He once got into trouble by taking the Old Guard past the Palace at a trot. We understood this to be because he was lunching at Hurlingham (where he was to play polo that afternoon). The guard normally walks past the Palace, but today the trumpeter had difficulty in sounding. Anyway, a very important person within the Palace noticed. A telephone call to Hyde Park Barracks put an end to polo that day and for a number of days afterwards. We saw quite a lot of him during the next week or so. And that was our gain.

The adjutant's successor, when the former took over my squadron, was also strict and efficient. Riding out onto the Bayswater Track in his blues, red-striped breeches and shining boots, astride a quality black horse of his own, I really believe that no more elegant a horseman could ever have been found. He also rode in steeplechases. But elegance and horsemanship were but a part, for he was later to become Secretary of State for War, Minister of Defence and a well-loved High Commissioner in both Nigeria and Malaysia. A fellow trooper was filled with admiration for this officer when he had to accompany him as his driver.

'Smokes these Balkan Sobranies,' he told us. 'What smell like camel dung and tram tickets, but cost a couple bob each. He never took more than half a dozen puffs from any of them! Chucked 'em away nine-tenths whole!'

He admired that. So did his audience. They loved what they called 'a proper toff'. One day when he was equitation officer, and when the Riding School was choc-a-bloc with horses cantering round, 'right hand to right hand', and somewhat raising the dust, he ascended onto the balcony. It was fully expected that some staccato criticism would soon be unleashed. Nothing of the sort. 'Shades of Dettingen and Waterloo!' was all he was heard to murmur.

Quite a different sort of officer had transferred from the Foot Guards, a boldish thing to do we then thought. But he too was an exceptional horseman and is to this day as good a man to hounds as you could find. It is written that the late Jack Gittins said of him: 'Every time I follow him down to draw some covert, he jumps it!' He became Master of the same pack of foxhounds for a quarter of a century, is an outstanding judge of hunters and a driving force behind the National Light Horse Breeding Society. He once told me that the only thing that alarmed him, on transferring from the Foot Guards as a very junior officer, was his Life Guard soldier-servant. 'Bowler hat, blue suit, rolled umbrella – terrifying!'

The Life Guards were proud of their officers. An ex-Welsh miner, a dear in most respects, once announced, after a few pints, that we were 'lions led by lambs'. He must have wished he had never spoken, tough as he was. In The Life Guards Christmas was Christmas indeed. Guards were, of course, mounted as usual, but 'the brick was hung' and, guards aside, discipline was relaxed. But thanks almost entirely to our officers putting their hands in their pockets, Christmas dinner was an occasion indeed. Turkey and all the trimmings, and so many crates of beer for so few men (roughly half the regiment went on leave, leaving the other half to look after the horses and various guards) that one wondered how it could all be consumed. But it was.

At Christmas dinner the NCOs waited on the soldiers. There was none of that, as I have always thought, abnormal and obsequious business of the officers doing it, an inverted sort of sucking up. Officers in paper hats handing round the food and drink would have been beyond the imagination horrible. But toasts were drunk and, for a few minutes, there existed a relationship that matched that which still obtains on large, well-run country estates. The Commanding Officer, who ranked a lot higher than God, had ridden the winner of the Grand Military Gold Cup. Behind him were gathered in their frock coats those of his officers who were either not on leave or who had made a point of coming to London. They were horsemen all and worthy of the description. The oldest soldier, who happened to be the Commanding Officer's groom (his brother was currently RSM of the 4th/7th Dragoon Guards), proposed their health and the officers responded. It gives some idea of the soldier's outlook when I say that they referred to their officers by their Christian names.

It was with something of dread that I first attended the ceremony of 'Hanging the Brick' at Knightsbridge – a real brick from Hougoumont Farm on the battlefield of Waterloo – which was kept in a velvet-lined box with its own gold chain. Once hung, probably by some retired RCM, discipline was slightly relaxed for those who had had to remain on duty in order to allow others away on leave. But Hanging the Brick turned out to be quite different from the normal organised bonhomie. The holiday atmosphere actually managed to make itself felt in that then austere old-fashioned barracks. I have since spent Christmas amid the ploughed-up plains of Northern France, twice in North African deserts and another in Algeria. I have spent Christmas in Germany and twice on liners in mid-ocean. But for my part the Life Guards did it – as with so many other things – best.

But from the sublime to the subterranean. Chaff was fed in considerable quantities and we were the folk who chopped it. Chaff-cutting fatigue was at any time bad, but on a hot summer's afternoon it was an earthly hell. It took place in a cellar into which you could peer, if you wanted to, through the iron grill beside the Knightsbridge entrance to the barracks. The fatigue began at 2 p.m. on Mondays and ended when the job was finished. All the time one breathed a dust that resembled pale grey fur. Oats were crushed at the same time, which entailed carrying sacks of whole oats down the steep, stone steps and the many more, though lighter, sacks of crushed oats up again. A sack of whole oats weighed twenty stone. Today I believe one can only require an employee to carry a hundredweight, a difference of twelve stone per sack, or in other words, over a ton less during an afternoon.

Also, of course, the trusses (not bales) of hay were carried down and the chaff – its lightness a comparative joy – brought up. Although this fatigue was not a punishment – not officially – I used to think that the Penal Battalion of the French Foreign Legion can have had few more irksome tasks. At the end of it we were coughing, bloodshot-eyed and really filthy. Strong, fit boys would wash (in cold water, since Monday was not a bath night and, even then, the only hot taps were in the bath block) and go unashamedly to bed after six hours non-stop, having most probably been on some sort of guard the previous night.

Another fatigue I could have done without was NCOs' mess on Sundays. Scrubbing their floors or, worse, washing up the eggy remains of their breakfasts, lowered my morale and raised my gorge as did nothing else. But then the Church party would come swinging back into barracks to some splendid march, white plumes blowing in the breeze, helmets and swords flashing, and I was saved by the bell – or the bull. And of course time and again by the horses.

If things seemed very fairly awful sometimes, there were always the horses. I suppose it was that they brought an atmosphere of the country. Also they are above human worries. All through my recruits' course I was incredibly lucky in being allotted the lovely Henrietta (B102). She was never taken for guards because she never got used to wearing a sheepskin. It tickled, so I had her always. She had a wonderfully smooth trot. As we were not allowed stirrups for nine-tenths of the time, this was unbelievably important. After a prolonged spell of being told to 'Change horses one up, Double!' (which meant jumping off your own horse and vaulting onto the one in front for a couple of turns round the school until you had ridden every horse in the ride), one came fully to appreciate a comfortable trot like Henrietta's. I paid her frequent visits and by no means only when in need of comfort. The atmosphere surrounding horses is at least wholesome. Some troop horses would automatically lay their ears back at the approach of man. Henrietta would cock hers and, resting her jowl on my shoulder, breathe a heavy sigh. 'Cheer up,' she said – and then she would take just enough of my sleeve between her teeth to include the smallest possible amount of flesh.

But if some moments were just not far off unbearable, there were many more that were tremendous. Few things, surely, could have been more exciting for a would-be cavalryman, fresh from a school desk, Pythagoras and Latin unseens, than mounted troop drill in Windsor Great Park. Mounted troop drill to the bugle (trumpets in barracks, bugles in the field and it was as well to know each call) could be a bit hair-raising at first. If you kept your eye on the centre guide and knee-to-knee with your neighbours, you were all right. Galloping about the Park was so much preferable to sinking into the Slough of Despond with poor old Bunyan. And a mounted attack on the Bailiff's Lodge was enormous fun at eighteen.

Again, there were the regimental sports and it was tremendous to be told that I, a mere recruit, might enter for the mounted wrestling! The corporal of horse who gave me permission must have had his tongue in his cheek. Competitors rode bareback and circled each other, waiting for the word 'go', about twenty of us. Then we just rode into the fray and the last man to be left 'twixt mane and tail would be the winner – and what a warrior! I gleefully kicked the horse allotted me (not, I am glad to say, the lady-like Henrietta) into the mêlée, chock-full of confidence. I found myself immediately on my back amongst a flurry of hooves after the sort of fall where the head follows the rest, which can be worse than the headfirst variety. A giant hand had seized my shirt collar from behind and pulled me over my horse's quarters as if I had been a little child. My ears sang. Yet it took no time to realise that unless I moved elsewhere with alacrity, death or injury by trampling was imminent. But it is a miracle how horses avoid bodies if they can. Sometimes, going fast in a race for instance, they cannot. Given a chance to avoid you they take it. I crawled clear.

There were happier moments when the tempo slowed down slightly. We sometimes played cricket on the lawn (mowed by a horse-drawn machine, the horse wearing large leather boots) in front of the officers' mess. After which we might graze the horses (instead of whisping them) during the hour of evening stables, beneath the flowering chestnuts that bordered the barrack square. The grass can have had little value beneath those trees, but it was a bit of 'Doctor Green' for the horses and comparatively restful ('comparatively' because grazing horses are never still) for us.

Whisping was warming work, but grooming with body-brush and curry-comb is perhaps one of the hardest tasks connected with the care of horses. Correct grooming incorporates, or should, the vigorous brushing of the legs. You squat or bend down and rub really hard in an unnatural position. (Which is why so many civilian horses' legs are filthy and, partly, why they get cracked heels.) This correct grooming (an NCO's jaundiced eye permanently ensuring that it was indeed correct) was occasionally eased for me by the presence of the regimental band. This sometimes played during the morning on the square. Nothing takes me back to my early days at Windsor as does Wagner's prelude to the third act of *Lohengrin*. One could hear the band practising upstairs in the band room even when they were not blaring it out gloriously on the square. But I am sure I applied more 'elbow grease' because of its stirring rhythms.

I discovered so many things. If you are not frightened of a horse, he probably will not be frightened of you. Once when on night guard I had to go into a stall several times to a horse that persisted, all through the small hours, on getting his rugs hanging over to one side. I would straighten them at first with a strongish pull, but finally I had to take them off and rug him up anew. During the look round before being relieved, I saw for the first time that there was a notice on his heel post, white letters on a red board, THIS HORSE IS DANGEROUS. Only one named man was apparently allowed near him in the stable. I had gone in to him several times all unawares and found him more patient than an old cow. Indeed, I had been the impatient one. Had I gone to him in fear and trembling with the 'Whoa there, lad, there's a lovely boy!' attitude, I might have been kicked into the middle of next week. And deserved to be.

Came the summer with a gentle warmth spreading into the Park, watering order (early daily exercising of horses not on guard) was carried out in daylight. The branches of the London-blackened old trees suddenly sprouted youthful greenery. Banks of daffodils were replaced with acres of tulips. Dull sentry-go outside the officers' mess became interesting. The Season was getting under way and there was gaiety in the air.

It was the Silver Jubilee year of King George V and Queen Mary. May 10th was not far away with its service in St Paul's Cathedral and processions to and from with escorts to be provided by the Life Guards. Busy as it made life, I was thankful that chance should have had us stationed in London that year, while the Blues languished at Windsor.

Rarely did one hear a word in favour of the deb dance, but I was soon to become unashamedly a fan. Every night – but *every* night that one was not on guard duty – I dined in some kind person's house, usually within a mile of the barracks. Then on somewhere to dance to the music from the films of Fred Astaire and Ginger Rogers; and tunes such as 'Zing! Go the strings of my heart!' and the carefree 'Anything Goes'.

Although shortage of sleep was inevitable, I was never sick throughout the two and half years I spent in the regiment. As for being tired, it is odd now to think that I always felt genuinely sorry when the band played Noël Coward's 'The Party's Over Now' before we were brought down to earth by 'John Peel'. For walking back to barracks in white tie and tails through lamplit London, my fun would be only slightly marred by the knowledge that so often I would be parading for King's in about five hours' time. Me personally that is. No valets or grooms to turn me out. Not yet awhile.

Several girls I knew and liked were 'doing the Season'. Joining in their fun was all pleasure as far as I was concerned and I was lucky to be asked. I had no girl friend: if I was in love with anybody, it was with Frances Farmer in *Come and Get It!* at the London Pavilion, a film about a Canadian logging camp. I went to see it ten times. As for those deb dances, I was on several occasions given a lift home by my officers from places as far afield as Ham House or Kings Walden Bury in Hertfordshire, where the Jack Harrisons give the very best of parties. One summer I had no way of getting to the latter place. Hearing this, Charlie Carlos-Clark, who was not even going himself, provided a car (a Rolls) with a chauffeur to take me there and back. I had just been introduced to him at some luncheon party – I did not even know him, nor he me. I thought this gesture was as kind in its way as Major McCreery lending me a polo pony for a Tidworth Rally and Major Christopher lending me a horse to ride round the hunter trial course when I was a boy. They were all old enough to be my father and had never met me before; but they knew that boys have no money (or perhaps should have no money) and their hearts were kind. Much later on, sister Molly once asked me at the eleventh hour to join a party at the Café de Paris. I was quite often called in as 'an extra man' and at that age did not mind one bit. The following morning, during stables, a young officer, after a period of obvious deliberation, suddenly edged up to me and asked: 'Wasn't it you I saw last night with five of the most beautiful women in London?' My troop leader at the time eventually married one of them, Hilary Charles, though he was not the subaltern in question. Marguerite Strickland was another. I forget the other two, but Molly was already well-known for her looks as well as her drawings in *The Bystander* and every time she entered the Four Hundred, Tim Clayton, the band leader, would play 'Harlem' because he knew it was her favourite tune at the time.

A contemporary of mine was Michael Matheson. (He was to retire from the Army as a colonel of Royal Artillery, but at that time he, too, was a trooper.) Because we started in different squadrons, we did not meet for over a year, which was a sorry waste of time. However, his presence was to lighten my outlook beyond telling. He had such a ready sense of the ridiculous – as for example, occasions like winning a case of fish knives in some mounted sports competition. He had a straightforward approach and a determination to stick it out till he got to Sandhurst. I could have been swayed, sometimes, the other way (during, say, a week of doing orderly corporal in London) had I had a weaker friend. But Michael dismissed any notions of failure. We became 'half-sections'.

There was a shortage of men in the regiment, which I found difficult to understand having had to join a waiting list before being summoned. However, a day's hunting such as Michael and I sometimes enjoyed made a welcome change from King's, barrack and night guards, duties that on top of the extra numbers of escorts were recurring very regularly – too regularly for some, who simply pushed off for a while and became AWOL or eventually even deserters. Considering the pay they were getting, you could hardly blame them. But their absence scarcely made the hearts of the dutiful grow fonder. One morning the Commanding Officer addressed the regiment from the balcony of the Riding School. He told us that things would get better. After a while, they did.

It was during my second term at Windsor that I was given promotion more important to me than anything under that heading was to follow. I was made an 'acting unpaid lance-corporal'. In *Slim* by Ronald Lewin, the Field-Marshal is reported as having said this was the most important and *hardest to obtain* of all promotions. I wish to second that. For it meant much more than simply having a couple of stripes and a crown sewn onto the sleeves of my tunic and wearing gold aiguilettes on my left shoulder in full kit.

Never again would I do sentry-go, getting out of bed at a quarter to one on a frosty morning in order to patrol on foot the deserted Horse Guards. Between the two locked gates, never again would I pray for the chimes of Big Ben to come crashing musically down empty Whitehall, signalling for me a return to bed at 3 a.m. till I must leave it again at 6. No more night guard either, which was as bad, fighting off sleep in warm stables with many of the horses prostrate and snoring all round, my friends overhead similarly engaged. No more would I have to carry in my arms heavy, warm, ammonia-pungent manure from stable to yard in the cold dark of Reveillé stables. Nor would I ever again have to show out the horses (we frequently 'did' three) which I had groomed to some totally unsympathetic NCO. After all, if he *wanted* to find a horse dirty, he had but to rub his immaculate white-gloved fingers against the hair over the croup or, with a ticklish character, the belly, or close to the mane behind the ears before the inevitable: 'Take him back in and this time *groom* him! He'll die laughing if you tickle his ribs like that.' Which meant that instead of being able to get on cleaning the tack (horse first, kit second, a sequence, incidentally, that I have failed after hunting to impress on any girl groom), you started grooming all over again and had to clean the kit in your free time. But it certainly made for glossy coats with the horses being whisped for at least twenty minutes at evening stables as well. We used to say ten minutes was long enough, but thought it wise to keep it to ourselves.

One of the main benefits of promotion was membership of the WOs' and NCOs' mess, with respect, streets ahead of some officers' messes in which I have since been briefly housed while on various courses. The members were genuinely interested in horses, the horses they worked with and knew, why some were good doers and others not, the good rides, the less good, temperaments, the minor ailments – it was all part of the invaluable early training in horsemastership. But the extra comfort was more than acceptable. (A memory of the troopers' mess was of a soldier at our corner table who had finished his meal and wished to leave. He stood on a bench, placed a boot beside my plate, stepped onto the further bench and departed. He left a squashed horse-dropping on the table.)

In my new home on a winter's morn you could have a quick look through the day's cards in the *Sporting Life* after breakfast before a blazing fire. As a trooper you had only the barrack room to go back to from the dining hall, only your bed to sit on in the unlikely event of there being no parade or fatigue to claim you. To sum up, I think it cannot be far wrong to say a trooper had one hell of a life, an NCO a very pleasant one. I found a wide gulf between the two existences. In other words there were strong incentives to promotion for those who did not fear responsibility.

When I became a dutyman I had to relinquish Henrietta to some fortunate recruit, due to her old-established dislike of a sheepskin. Instead I took on a rather plain (if he will forgive me) but good horse, Bill (B17). There came a day when he and I should have won the NCO's jumping and the dummy thrusting as well. But Bill, like one or two other rather common horses I have since known, enjoyed putting on a show of shying at things of which he was not really in the least frightened. For the first time in his career he decided to hang away from the 'charge dummy' as if he had never seen such a thing, thus mischievously ensuring that my sword could only prick it. Again he treated the first and smallest obstacle of the show jumping course with utter disdain, going clean over the rest. They say never blame your horse, it is always the rider's fault. Is it? That was the competition in which Michael Matheson was second and won his case of fish knives. In the afternoon I won a cake dish for being third out of forty-seven starters in the sack race. I gave it to a married trooper who, incidentally, thought nothing of bicycling home to London every evening (he had a staff job) and back to Windsor by Reveillé.

Conversation between officer and soldier was only conducted in the presence of the troop corporal, who acted, I suppose, as a sort of interpreter. But during NCO's training we had what was known as a Tantivy over most of the obstacles in the Riding School field. The equitation officer led the way and we followed in single file, rather like modern foxhunting. In fact, exactly like modern foxhunting, because horses refused in front of you (though no one actually cut in) and at the end I found myself further up the queue perhaps than was seemly. For all his faults, Bill did not know the word 'stop', so I may have slightly swallowed the poker. The equitation officer regarded me unsmilingly. My exhilaration began to ebb. 'Turn round,' he said, 'and go back the way we have come and jump *everything*. And this time *ride* your horse.' The rebuke went home for I thought I had ridden rather well. However, this meant, amongst other pleasures, a ditch towards with a bit of a drop and a small, but fixed triple bar with, of course, the nearest pole the highest of the three. Bill devoured it. For one thing this return journey was towards his stable and for me it was the reverse of punishment. It could even have been an intended kindness, though I rather doubt it.

After putting Bill in and seeing him right, Regimental Orders had it that I had passed my First Class Certificate of Education – about the first thing concerning that side of life I ever had passed. Much better, there was, in the adjoining letter-rack, an invitation to stay at Martley for the Ludlow Hunt Ball. And so, in 'plain clothes' and via Waterloo to the Berkeley, where there were sometimes friends and almost always acquaintances who had spent the afternoon on the racecourse.

Not long after this my section won the inter-troop competition. This was an enjoyable affair of show jumping, rifle-shooting, and dummy-throwing. I was lucky in having some 'cut-and-thrust merchants' in my section, and, knee to knee between numbers one and three, Bill just had to keep straight. I believe the official accompaniment to a charge was 'a short, sharp shout'. My section, as we left the charge dummies swaying behind us, sounded as if a fox had been killed.

The carefree call of the trumpet rang out: 'Old soldiers to bed and young soldiers to school'; the more practical 'Fall in the picket and the guard'; and finally the rather ominous 'Fall in recruits'. Each followed the other without interval to mark 1400 hours in pre-war Windsor. As an NCO one could ignore the lot – and get some leave and go away hunting.

Back in London and riding down Constitution Hill on a fine autumn morning, the atmosphere of hunting hung comfortably in the air. With the prospect of a long weekend including the opening meet on Saturday, it was a fairly uncomplicated life provided you kept clean, alert, punctual – and your mouth shut. And I was now sometimes able to slip away from evening stables in the interval between the feed-tins being set on the floor behind each horse and the trumpet sounding 'Feed!' This small detail gave the necessary few minutes' start which made it possible for the young, fit and determined to catch the most suitable train from Waterloo. Few would believe, or have the misfortune to find out, how quickly, given a bit of luck, one can get from a Knightsbridge stable to a Pullman dining car at Waterloo using only the Underground and one's own legs. Yet exhilarating indeed were those Friday evening or Saturday midday dashes for freedom! Up to the washroom three steps at a time; on with the plain clothes, down to the yard five steps at a time; sprint to Knightsbridge Station, ignoring the cry of 'Stand clear of the doors'; run up the escalators at Waterloo; and a final wriggle through the closing iron gates onto the platform, with ticket-collectors protesting, whistles blowing, people running, flags waving and wheels already beginning to turn.

Then the sweet peace of dining, or lunching, on the train to Andover: Sandown Park, Brooklands and the familiar Stoneycastle Camp sliding astern while attentive waiters good-naturedly saw to one's needs. And so to beloved Hampshire, grinding to a squeaking, hissing halt at Basingstoke, then but a modest market town. To cries of 'Next stop Andover!' and slamming of doors, we jerked once more into motion to puff and clank through a countryside of slumbering beechwoods and almost stationary rivers, hairy old downland fences, a hare 'coming out abut the corn', a covey of partridges unalarmed at the train's passing and then the tall trees and water-cress beds of Hurstbourne. Finally the woods and fields that I knew so intimately, even a glimpse of our own copper beeches which sheltered the tennis court above the green curve of Andover Down. The unmatchable warmth of homecoming was strengthened by the grey-moustached porter and the ticket-collector, who actually appeared pleased to see one. ('Yes, sir, the Colonel's been poorly lately, but we hear he has taken a turn for the better and your visit will make him better still!' And I honestly believe they hoped it would.)

But the life of the orderly corporal was not easy. When a class of recruits was finally 'passed off', one might have thought that there would be a few more men for duty. Oddly enough, not so. They vanished into staff jobs. From the cook-house to the messes, to the saddlers, to the pharmacy, to the Riding School, to the tailor's shop, to the armourers. It left the orderly corporal tearing his hair as to how to find men for guards, for which he was initially entirely responsible. Parade states were just a nightmare to me and the fear of putting a foot – or getting a figure – wrong, thereby incurring 'a week's extra orderly corporal' as a punishment, was a very real one. It was perfectly lovely to be able to hand over at the end of the week.

After which it was an extra pleasure to get out of barracks on a horse. A newly-joined subaltern had complained that the horse he rode on Riding School 'played up'. He said he wanted someone to ride it for at least an hour beforehand. How an old-time riding master would have handled the matter (exceptionally good horsemen and dashing G.R. though this sub-altern was), one can but guess. However, I was the beneficiary for I volunteered. As long as the officer was on Riding School, I was able to spend the early mornings riding alone in the park or hacking round Chelsea and the districts either side of Sloane Street. Not very entertaining? Far better than Reveillé stables! But against the charm of freedom, there were depressing aspects so early in the morning. The small gilt chairs stacked high for collection outside a house in Cadogan Square where one had been dancing but three hours earlier. The steps being scrubbed and the brasses being polished by maids of houses wherein one's contemporaries still slept. A suicide being hauled out of the Serpentine, a female one, somehow worse than a male. Tramps sleeping (or dead?) on benches, covered in old newspapers. The collection of the dustbins. It was a side of London never seen by civilised mortals who rose at 'a gentlemanly hour'.

The most wretched thing I had to do was to take some horses to be slaughtered. There were occasional 'casting parades' when horses which were considered to have passed their usefulness were detailed to be put down. There were, on this occasion, three of us in charge of six horses and we rode and led them to a slaughterhouse somewhere near the Caledonian Market. I thought it a ghastly waste as mine looked well and walked into his bridle. I had to wait to sign a form and they were already slabs of meat as in a butcher's shop before we were able to get away from the place. We were a rather shocked and sorrowful trio returning to Knightsbridge by Underground, bridles, saddles and blankets strapped together by the surcingle on our knees.

I derived a deal of enjoyment from *The Collected Works of Saki*. And I dare say I assumed some of the more sardonic side of my character from following so often the doings of that arrogant pair, Clovis Sangrail and Comus Bassington. But my other even happier discovery was *The Irish R.M.* Throughout the rest of my life, whenever I have picked up this classic by Edith Somerville and Martin Ross and at whatever page I have opened it, I have laughed at the very first sentence.

Although I personally preferred London to Windsor, the riding at Windsor was obviously superior. Mounted exercises in the Great Park never bored me. One day, while taking a mounted patrol from Forest Gate to Snow Hill, I saw some 'enemy' (white bands round caps) by the Prince Consort's Workshops. They failed to notice our presence, so we cantered away on a longish detour over the lovely turf, eventually rounding some trees to come in amongst their led horses. Nobody ever tried to take more uncooperative prisoners, but surprise was on our side and the timely arrival of an umpire saw to it that no lives were lost. I think that a mounted patrol was only supposed to 'see without being seen'. On that occasion, however, the opportunity for action seemed too good to miss and the umpire seemed happy.

Perhaps a slightly more romantic memory of the Great Park was when I was detailed late one evening to take back from an exercise on Chobham Ridges those due for guard duty next day. It was dark by the time my party reached the Park and I therefore decided to follow Queen Anne's Ride along its whole length. As we trotted swiftly over the grass the only sounds were the wind in the trees, the jingle of accoutrements, and the occasional clack of shoe. The darkness and silence gave us the impression of moving faster than we were, maybe momentarily through a past century in 'mid-thigh boots and riding cloaks'. Then twinkling lights ahead of the Royal Borough; recruits took our horses and 'did' them for us that night while we were allowed to go straight to our messes for a hot meal. Having one's horse 'done' for one was an almost unique experience, the rarest of luxuries.

As regards exercises, the best fun by far was when the Regiment rode from Windsor to Petworth. Though we did not know it, we were to take part in what were to be the last horsed cavalry manoeuvres ever to be held in this country. We were encamped in Petworth Park, presumably because our Commanding Officer was Lord Leconfield's brother, for the rest of the cavalry were quartered elsewhere. On our first day there and with the sun shining bravely, squadrons were split up into troops, which were then taken on a gate-shutting exercise. We went our separate ways across country to give as many as possible of the soldiers and horses an opportunity of opening and shutting a few gates, an essential country accomplishment not normally taught at Windsor or in London. On our way back into Petworth itself, our troop leader let us into a yard behind the inn which stands just outside the park wall. We sat on our horses knee to knee, the sun warm on our khaki backs. Presently, pint after foaming pint was handed out through a rear window – at least twenty of them, and all at the behest and expense of our troop officer, who, so far as I know, had never looked at or spoken directly to any of us and who even now continued to run true to form. Not that any of us liked him less for that. As we rode through Petworth back to camp, women came out of their houses and held up baskets of eating apples for us to help ourselves.

At Petworth, too, there came a dawn when pink ground mists near the lake beautified the sunrise as the regiment headed north to take part in an exercise. If Reveillé and morning stables had been a bit rugged, this, for me, was very near total happiness. Just after the war I once led the 12th Lancers out of Colchester northwards along the Stoke-by-Nayland road. Turning round in the turret I could see a long line of armoured cars following fast in single file. Splendidly impressive. But it could not compare with the sheer *beauty* of The Life Guards in a column of half-sections, stretching back over a mile that summer's morn of 1936, black horses knee deep in the ground mist, the early sun just picking out the highly polished items of equipment. And the horses came in silence.

We rode bareback three times a day at Petworth and led another horse down to the lake to water. There would be deer grazing peacefully beyond the beeches from which came the murmur of wood pigeons. One horse nearly trod on a mallard duck which waddled out from under its hoofs before taking wing. 'Mind that bloody partridge,' yelled an NCO, adding that almost daily advice, 'and *ride* your bloody horse!' It all added to the fun. As did the appearance of Lord Leconfield's hounds being walked out from their kennels as we dismounted at the lake's edge. What a pity there was no Lionel Edwards or Munnings there to paint the scene, for no one will see the like again. There would never be anything approaching the same number of horses for one thing.

One day all the infantry were suddenly removed from the camp by convoys of buses. Rumour had it, correctly, that they were bound for Palestine. The Life Guards, The Royal Scots Greys, the Queen's Bays and the 4th Hussars were left alone to carry out an exercise amongst themselves. The sole drawback to this otherwise enjoyable romp was that Life Guards' tack was of burnished steel, polished leather throughout, and polished brass fittings, whereas that of the line cavalry (with, we thought, practical common sense) was all in good old soap and oil. After a wet night-march it may be imagined the extra toil needed to get *our* accoutrements back into shape again. There was no winking an eye because of the unusual circumstances, no delaying of the normal and therefore rigorous inspections. Our horse-furniture was expected to be just as clean as if we were at Knightsbridge. We were saved by first, the sun, which helped dry out the leather and secondly, because the local soil under the trees above the lake was better than brick-dust for removing rust, being of an even finer sand.

I now had a horse called Charlie (B54). I had ridden him on King Edward VIII's parade. Like Henrietta, he had more quality than most and could genuinely get a move on. Luckily I had had no trouble on the parade, even during the gallop past. But since then he had hooked it good and proper during an ordinary scheme in the Great Park. In spite of a Household Cavalry bit (we were shortly moving to London so had recently changed back from the 9th Lancer pattern) or possibly because of it, I had only managed to stop him by steering him towards the unjumpable ditch and very high hedge on the perimeter of the Royal Lodge. I later discovered he had been in the Household Brigade Drag stables, but 'no one could hold him'. Nor could I. Not that morning anyway. In fact, I think Charlie must have been a goodish horse. One morning on manoeuvres I was sent alone to a flank to report if there were signs of enemy in Hawkhurst. It was clear, so I rode back a different way and popped over a small gate, which was tied top and bottom with string, to get onto the Petworth road. Low as it was, it did have five bars. Just at that moment my troop leader, with troop, came into view just ahead. He halted the troop and waited for me. He even addressed me.

'Did you *jump* that gate?' he asked.

'Yes, sir,' I said. He eyed me and my horse in silence and without expression. Was he about to tick me off or would he say 'Well done!'? Neither. He was no doubt deciding that Charlie might be the horse for him to take away to hunt next season instead of, or as well as, Percy, which he was riding.

'Walk march!' he said. I fell into place and away we all went. With respect, I think Charlie was a tiny bit 'loco'. He would shake his head and shake his head. Waiting for the King to arrive that morning in the Park I thought he would nearly shake it off altogether. It was as if he had an earwig or ants in his ears. But he was not mad, not, at least, when I rode him in the musical chairs competition at the sports. We were out fourth chair, because by then he had already learned enough of what was required of him not to do it. (For the first three chairs, he was superb.) In the Handy Hunter class he refused to be led over a pole for which you had to dismount in order to place it on the ground. Perhaps he felt ill, for soon afterwards he began to go to nothing for no apparent reason. After trying various things, the powers that be had him put down. Being young, distraught and very fond of him, I asked for a hoof to make an inkpot. I was told that he was 'riddled through and through with TB'.

In Sussex he had been grand, especially when we had to gallop after some Bays' horses that crossed our front somewhere near the Royal Sussex golf course. A soldier in my section came dashing out of a lane with a line head-kit round his shoulders shouting that he had a prisoner. 'He wouldn't dismount so I pulled the bridle off too! He's back there with his arms round his dobbin's neck, if you want him.' I told him to go back and drop it on the verge where he could get it, then join me. We galloped in pursuit of the others. 'For God's sake keep off the fairway!' I yelled. It was nearly as good as a hunt.

A hint that mechanisation of the cavalry was nigh (the 11th Hussars and 12th Lancers were already in armoured cars – the 12th had been in them for eight years) was that John Knebworth's signals troop of the Bays was already 'mounted' in little Austin Sevens, which, I noted in my diary, 'Were driven flat out everywhere and especially over hump-back bridges!'

Otherwise my only memory of personalities is of Neville Crump (who was to train no less than three Grand National winners) riding at the head of his troop of 4th Hussars. The edge of a blue bird's-eye scarf just showed above the collar of his mackintosh.

In the evenings, when we pegged down in quiet meadows and the horses were munching, muzzles deep down in their white canvas feed-bags, one carried one's mess-tin to some log or gate on which to consume the hot meal of the day – tepid and tasting of soot, but welcome. There was something extraordinarily wholesome and satisfying about it all.

During the lull at Petworth, I managed a weekend at Bognor Regis, famous then as the place where King George V had recuperated from illness. I stayed with my mother's eldest and favourite sister (and my favourite aunt by, in racing parlance, a distance). My diary says that 'we bathed in the sea from the Cambridges' house in almost foreign warmth and sunshine and watched county cricket in the afternoon. Then an evening swim followed by watching three plays of Noël Coward's in one performance at the local theatre. On Sunday we swam in the morning, played tennis in the afternoon and bathed again before tea. I was back in camp before midnight.'

Alas, the cavalry had to return to barracks as suddenly as the infantry had left camp for Palestine. Foot and mouth had broken out in Sussex and put the kibosh on our fun. So the Life Guards went by special train instead of riding home as I had hoped. Looking out of my carriage window, I could see all the horses' tails streaming in the wind from the sides of the waggons along the length of the train. There was a tremendous atmosphere of hustle and bustle when we de-trained at Windsor Southern Railway station. The place was jam-packed with tall soldiers and their black horses. The place echoed to the sound of hoofs, shouted commands, hissing steam and the crash of ramps for unloading. I never saw such verve. The squadrons lined up without fuss on the Datchet road, the Castle towering overhead, then rode in column of half-sections to Combermere Barracks, as shiningly clean as if riding out of there on a Monday morning.

Back at Windsor there immediately followed a horse inspection. In spite of covering many miles, they looked well. Public duties in London were only a month or so away. A saddlery inspection was followed by an arms parade, for which we dressed in 'best khaki with two caps' – khaki and red (we sported the former less glamorous model for the occasion and carried the other) best slacks over right arm – and, as Trooper 'Smudger' Smith put it, 'Mess tins at the trail with hoof-picks, burnished, at the high port'! After which we were told that the Inspector-General of Cavalry (General Mike Houston, an 11th Hussar who once commanded the 12th Lancers) had written a personal letter to our Commanding Officer, to say how excellently well the regiment had done and 'how quickly it had moved'. 'This', wrote our Commanding Officer, 'is high praise from one not given to praise unless deserved. So I think we can be satisfied.'

I have already told how Henrietta could not abide a sheepskin. But the Jubilee summer called for extra duties such as the Saturday escorts and it was therefore ordained that she must wear one again. She was needed for King's guard in order to release more reliable horses for escorts. She had been ridden on the escort for Prince George and Princess Marina. I had had to get up before six to ride her round and round the school to settle her down. With a sheepskin on she bucked, bucketed and hoisted her quarters nearly all the time. But she managed her escort duty without mishap. It was Trooper Wakelin who was detailed to take her to Whitehall with the guard, though in the event it was she who took him.

He told me that while the guard was riding down Constitution Hill, Henrietta was 'cantering backwards' down the tan between the road and Green Park. Their progress was much the same past Carlton House Terrace, 'missing most of the trees'. I understood that he got her into the Horse Guards 'all of a piece' and somewhere near the guard!

After that, the lady rejoined the recruits' ride – and never went on public duties again. I regaled my daughter with a doubtless tedious account of this little episode on a very sunny afternoon nearly forty years later. We were en route for her wedding in the Guards Chapel. Going down Constitution Hill I remembered Henrietta. I also thought the story might take her mind off the immediate nerve-racking future. (Nerve-racking for me, anyway – would, for example, the bridesmaids have been picked up from all the right places and delivered in time? Would anyone turn up? So many 'ifs'.) We were a little early, so our chauffeur slowly circled the Victoria Memorial two or three times while I told her of Henrietta. Unnecessary, of course, for a calmer bride one could not have accompanied – and it turned out to be a very beautiful wedding.

On the whole, the troop horses were extraordinarily well-mannered and long-suffering. Yet when I was on my very last 'King's' I had arranged to be photographed in full review order riding the good-looking Andy. Mr Field, the quiet and mild-mannered photographer who had 'taken' the regiment for many years, came to the Horse Guards especially. Just as all was ready, there came considerable sounds of commotion from Whitehall. Percy (he had been hunted during the winter months by my troop leader) was playing up in the street and napping, refusing to go back into the sentry-box. Compared with foxhunting, box duty in Whitehall was evidently not on. And as anyone knows who rides horses, standing still for any length of time is not their favourite pastime. I sometimes marvelled how the box horses could stand still for an hour at a time. Perhaps they went to sleep?

But it was my last chance of having my photograph taken 'in the kit' with the typical London background of War Office pillars and the Duke of Cambridge's mounted statue. Also Mr Field could not be expected to wait for ever. So I got onto Percy and the sentry finished his hour on Andy. Percy was still in a high old state of nerves. If in the photograph his head is too high and his ears are back, at least I have my picture. The London evening papers were full of the episode. There were photographs and a headline 'Guardsman Bolted With'. Bolted? That would have been something in crowded Whitehall. They must have been hard up for news.

At last the time came when I was eligible to apply for a commission. How anxiously I waited to hear whether my squadron leader would approve my application; and after that whether my Commanding Officer would agree. It was all very well for some to suggest I need not worry. I worried. But so far, so good. I eventually heard that I was to attend for an interview with the General Officer Commanding London District, General Sergison-Brooke. It was then discovered that I had not quite served the necessary six months as an NCO. So the adjutant suggested that I wrote on the form in question '24 weeks' i.e. 6 months of 28 days each. Then he countersigned it. In such diverse ways did our officers help us.

Nervous though I was, the general made my interview with him nothing but a pleasure. I returned to Knightsbridge feeling inches taller and full of confidence. But . . . In those good days cavalry officers enjoyed two months' hunting leave. When the day came for the document to be signed by a field officer, there was no such officer available. But a recommendation for a commission was only made half-yearly. Thus, incredibly, I missed this particular stage, being informed by an embarrassed and sympathetic orderly room corporal-of-horse that I 'must serve a further six months'. And so it was.

At that time in the pervading conditions, six months seemed a lifetime. Apart from mere disappointment and feeling of anti-climax, there was loss of seniority to consider, not that I cared a fig for that. What weighed in my mind were all the slips 'twixt cup and lip in the necessarily extra-strict and specialised London soldiering. Much better men than I had been reduced to the ranks for, in my view, very little reason. So every day was a challenge and six months an age to go without putting a foot wrong.

That was a long winter, at the end of which red tape decreed that the whole rigmarole must start again. I was on leave though more than happy to clean up my 'reds' and travel to attend at my own expense when called for a second interview with the General. It was to be an interview that lasted about one minute.

'Hullo!' said the general. 'But I have *seen* you!? What's gone wrong?'

'I don't know, sir,' I lied.

'You were at Stowe weren't you? Had they started the clay pigeon club in your day?'

'No, sir.'

'Hadn't it started?' He tapped his blotter with a pen. 'Pity,' he said, 'pity!' Then: 'Well, Bishop, you already know that I can't promise anything. The vacancies are few and the competition tremendous.'

He stood up, came round his desk and held out his hand. 'But I'll do my best for you,' he said. 'Goodbye. Good luck.'

And thanks to this (and perhaps that the hunting season was over) I was eventually informed that I was to proceed to the R.M.C. the following term.

The day arrived, therefore, when I took my leave of the Life Guards, shaking hands all round the long barrack room before catching a train for Andover. It was no figment of the imagination that my right hand still ached slightly when I reached home about two hours later. I think it had all been a bit too arduous, although often not unpleasantly so, for me to have a lump in my throat. But relieved, as of course I was, to be on the next rung of the ladder, I nevertheless loved the regiment with a love that only the regular soldier – and not all of them – would understand. It has survived and I still plan my occasional visits to Messrs Cox's and King's to coincide with the Changing. From the steps (Waterloo Place) I watch the new guard arrive, go and cash my cheque (or plead with the section manager), then watch the old guard riding up the Approach Road and away down the Mall. As I left the barracks I thought of all the horses I was leaving, so many of which I and my comrades-in-arms knew intimately and of which we were genuinely fond. For example, I never saw Henrietta again.

The Life Guards set standards for me which nothing could ever match. From what I have seen very recently and at close quarters, they still do. The Life Guards left me with the conviction that 'nothing could compare'. 'Once a Life Guard, always a Life Guard.'

4

In and Out of Battle

Sandhurst Tim found somewhat disenchanting, remarking that his time there was the only period of his life to which he did not look back with pleasure. Most of his fellow cadets were three years younger than he, and only just out of school. After his time in the Life Guards their company proved both immature and unsophisticated. Fortunately John Mogg (later to become a much-decorated fighting soldier, as well as a distinguished general) was the senior under officer of his company and, having gone through the ranks of the Coldstream Guards, understood and sympathised with his feelings, and persuaded him to abandon any question of quitting.

In the end, of course, he made a lot of friends (many for life) and, as ever, managed to get in much hunting, as well as riding some rather dubious horses in point-to-points. And in one of those bizarre situations – so prevalent in military life – found himself occupying, only six years later, his company commander's chair in the Old Building. Dick McCreery, a friend of his parents, had suggested that he should join the 12th Lancers (which he then commanded) along with John Clark-Kennedy and Edward Mann, also cadets at the R.M.C. In the late summer of 1938, with Neil Speke and Maurice Barker, fresh from their arduous studies at Cambridge, these young officers arrived at Tidworth, where the regiment was now commanded by Herbert Lumsden. It would seem – this was the time of Munich – that the authorities had at last decided to increase the Army and accordingly half a dozen subalterns were gazetted to the 12th (only four having joined during the previous five years).

Although there was hardly a year until the outbreak of hostilities, and although those young men were put through fairly rigorous training under the aegis of an outstandingly efficient and intelligent colonel – with Andrew Horsbrugh-Porter as their special mentor – there were many compensations. Despite mechanisation (which had taken place ten years previously and which had been wholly accepted and absorbed into regimental existence) officers still had a couple of chargers each, as well as a groom and a soldier servant, and most had other horses of their own. Much hunting and polo was available and encouraged, as well as the opportunity to ride in steeplechases.

The summer months of 1939 also saw a vast amount of rather splendid entertainments in London and elsewhere – perhaps there was a premonition that these pleasures would not recur – and la jeunesse *(whether* dorée, *or not) was certainly very constant in its assistance.*

Reading his recollections it is astonishing to find how much he crammed into these twelve months, including a somewhat reluctantly accepted mechanical course at Bovington, which he contrived to pass, despite the outside distractions. Owing to an injured shoulder and an impacted wisdom tooth he did not embark with the regiment for France in October 1939 saying that failing to do so 'was the end of the world, the most awful personal calamity.'

He need not have worried, as by arriving at the end of the year he missed two months of chilly and uncomfortable tedium before joining 'A' Squadron – commanded by Andrew Horsbrugh-Porter – in the insalubrious village of Fonquevillers, near Arras. We lived in this depressing place – apart from short periods of leave, and one or two 'alarms' that took us to the Belgian frontier – until May 1940, surrounded by the cemeteries of the previous conflict.

It was an exceptionally cold winter, the squadron leader did not welcome confined conditions and the days seemed interminable. The circumstances would have been insupportable without Tim.

In April he managed to get ten days' leave home.

I got back to the 12th Lancers in time for an alert and consequently an immediate move up to the Belgian frontier. This was both fun and interesting. It entailed a welcome change into rather more luxurious billets and was carried out in lovely spring weather. John Erne, about to command the North Irish Horse, had come over to pick up a few hints concerning armoured car soldiering and was temporarily second-in-command of the squadron. He had served in the Blues and was a great asset. He was the perfect buffer between ourselves and our fiery squadron leader. They made a good mixture at the top. But was the war starting in earnest at last? It was not. It was no time at all before we were trundling back to Fonquevillers.

Squadrons consisted of three troops, each of three armoured cars, with three more in squadron H.Q. But as the regiment was required to cover enormous frontages, a makeshift fourth troop was improvised in each squadron – most troops consisting of two cars only.

'A' Squadron was commanded by Andrew Horsbrugh-Porter, with John Erne, on temporary attachment, as second-in-command. Bruce Shand, Tim Bishop, Peter Arkwright and Andrew Roddick were the troop leaders. The

two latter were killed as was John Erne. Basil Hall was in charge of the transport.

We had not been there many days when I was called earlier than usual by my servant, Rowlands, on the morning of 10 May 1940, with the casual observation: 'I think there will be a jildi move, sir. Jerry's invaded Holland.' Here was another accurate forecast. We were packed up and, as a regiment, across the Belgian frontier by 1 p.m. the same day. 'Jildi' indeed when you think of it. We all had a glass or two of champagne at Toufflers and then crossed the frontier with Corporal Sims sounding the charge as each troop went past. About the last time I had heard that stirring call was when we were careering towards the first fence of our subalterns' race at the H.H. point-to-point. But I did not feel nostalgic. This was fun too.

Historians and many others have dealt *ad nauseam* with the disastrous campaign that followed. Perhaps, provided the lessons have been learned, it was best forgotten. Yet because it was all so dotty, for years afterwards the events of each day from 10 May to 1 June were imprinted in correct sequence on my memory. Time has softened the shock that did the imprinting. But the whole thing stands out quite clearly enough to this day.

We drove through Belgium on that beautiful morning, fêted all the way as 'les sauveurs'. It was "ullo Tommy!' 'Vive l'Angleterre!' and waving Union Jacks. When we had to slow down in order to pass through a town, the inhabitants swarmed onto the cars to push sprigs of lilac down the gun barrels. We had become a perambulating flower show through Tournai and Hal. We were, as we now all know, to come back through those very same places embarrassingly soon and under hideously different circumstances.

By the evening of 10 May we were at Grez Doiceau, where we ate a hot meal beside the château in the shelter of high trees. Tanks of the French Division Légère Motorisée moved clamorously and continuously past our HQ, tank after tank heading for the front, heightening our already high morale. Our outlook must have been helped by our total ignorance of the devastating fact that the total tank strength of the BEF was 97 while the Germans could field 6042! Even when the first enemy bombers went over, unopposed by Allied aircraft and ignoring the anti-aircraft fire, to drop their bombs unpleasantly close, my companion of the moment and I only exchanged smiles over our plates of stew. The black crosses on the bombers' wings were new to us.

'Did you hear how the bombs sort of scream? I'm told they put organ pipes on them. Wheee-WUMP! Positively childish!' On the first morning, 11 May,

Andrew sent me to liaise with the French on our right, to locate their HQ, determine their left and 'generally find out what the b---s are up to'. I found their HQ and more or less breezed in to see the general, meaning absolutely no disrespect but, I dare say, rather thinking of him as just a friendly old Frog. He was the reverse of friendly. I had to alter my approach. Here was a very pompous man indeed.

Be that as it may, it resulted in my getting all the information I needed immediately as, in the adjoining room, into which I was vocally catapulted, were his staff. They had not witnessed our meeting. Maps were laid out under my nose and I was quickly told everything I had come to find out. I did not think the general would appreciate my saying goodbye, so returned at once to the squadron with marked map and we moved on up to Tirlemont.

We entered this peaceful little town and halted. Andrew dispatched me to find a bakery; he thought it a good opportunity for getting fresh loaves. In answer to my enquiries, a pretty little girl of about ten years old was detailed by nodding, smiling parents to guide me. To cut out the necessity for words, she very sensibly took my hand in hers and led me back past my cars and the grinning faces in their turrets. I was willingly presented with bread, payment was refused and it was altogether the most charming bit of shopping I had ever known. As we were walking back, however, planes flew in low over the roofs. I saw people coming out of their houses, shading their eyes as they looked up. The planes were hidden by other houses. It seemed they were fighters which had started shooting up the landing ground. Hurray for the boys in blue, we said – and then saw the big black crosses on their sides as they zoomed over the chimneys. This was the first of a hundred such moments of disillusionment to come. These 'boys' belonged to the Luftwaffe and, for at least a fortnight, they always did.

We were heading for St Trond and Andrew yelled at me to get all the cars out of the town. I returned my adorable companion to her puzzled parents and ran back to my car. As we took the St Trond road, however, we at once met a formation of enemy bombers flying straight down the line of the road as it were to meet us, bombing as they came. The fact that they were not specifically aiming at us made not a ha'porth worth of difference. They were bombing the road, accurately, and we were on it. Moreover, owing to deep roadside ditches, we were unable to get off it. It was my first taste of something that was to become, over the next few years, almost commonplace. Great flaming spouts of black smoke and brown earth came leaping to meet us like huge, ugly trees in a death-dealing avenue, racing towards us. There was a deafening bang, the car rocked and shook, filling with choking fumes, while earth, stones and twigs rattled down into the turret and onto the back of my neck.

I presently poked a cautious nose over the turret's edge. My crew were all right, but a splinter had sliced off my wireless mast, base and all. As the smoke and dust drifted away, I was quite surprised to see that all the other crews seemed to be present and correct. But I was of course no longer in wireless communication with any of them, the *raison d'être* of an armoured car. More aircraft were pouring in. The RAF to the rescue? No (sinking down once more into the turret), black crosses on the lot and heading in over the town . . .

For what seemed hours we sat and watched Tirlemont systematically bombed to flaming ruins by relays of Stuka dive-bombers while their escorts of Messerschmitt 109 fighters, presumably because they had nothing from which to protect their bombers, came down to strafe, at low level, with their cannon and machine-gun fire. I had not imagined anything quite like *this*. We were sitting helplessly by, watching thugs murdering civilians, men, women and children regardless. As the Stukas dropped their 'sticks' of bombs they swooped up again like rooks on a windy day. Their escorts reminded me of ugly grey swallows, nightmare birds swooping about gleefully with none to say nay. My gunner and wireless operator watched in silence except for the word 'Bastards!' occasionally (and almost disbelievingly) whispered from time to time.

We knew the town to be clear of troops, but what of my little friend and her proud parents? What of the obliging kindly baker? Much of the place had already been reduced to a burning shambles. But we had to go on and as we did so I noticed that what seemed to be bundles of laundry had been thrown into the roadside ditches. Then I saw, with a crawling horror, legs and arms sticking out of the clothes and suddenly a green, upturned face. Dead men are bad enough; these were mostly women. The picnic period was over.

As soon as I could, I changed onto a car with a working wireless. This meant a new crew, but as every man in the squadron was first class and everybody knew everyone else, it made little, if any, difference. So I now had Trooper Lloyd instead of Trooper Cupples to drive me. After three days and nights of constant activity (the worst bits being the night marches when one could not know for certain just who was who on those dark and sinister roads,) I found myself with my three cars taking up a position in front of Louvain. It was 3 a.m. and my orders were to 'delay' the enemy.

Weary, but so needle-sharp from the sense of danger that we hardly noticed just how weary, we watched dawn break, fine and dry. This revealed some stationary civilian cars nearby, obviously immobilised, though not smashed, by very near misses from bombers. They stood at odd angles with shattered windscreens. One had a door hanging off its hinges. As the dawn light picked them out it also picked out their dead civilian occupants, sitting up as if ready to be driven on. One woman wore a fur coat. It did nothing at all to cheer us.

We had all been silent for a long time and the sun was up. Hallsworth, the gunner, and Brayshaw, the operator, were nodding off at my feet. In fact I kept gently kicking them to keep us all from going fast asleep. Then suddenly Trooper Lloyd spoke up from the driving seat: 'I thought,' he said, 'that these Jerries were meant to be 'ighly mobile.' Then, disgustedly, to anyone who might still be listening: 'They must be ---n' well walkin'.' He once more relapsed into silence.

At that moment three Bren carriers of the 13th/18th Hussars came rattling up from the rear, Derrick Martin in command. He had been sent up, believe it or not, to 'support' me. When the Germans appeared, I would delay them before withdrawing through the carriers, drawing the enemy onto their fire.

Perhaps I should here point out that the armoured car regiment was a reconnaissance unit. It was the eyes and ears of the Army. In a nutshell it accurately reported in detail the enemy's positions and progress, sometimes delaying them, but never getting involved. Being lightly armed it drew the enemy gradually onto its stronger elements – tanks, anti-tank guns and so on – and then withdrew behind the latter until the situation should once again become fluid. Very roughly it did the old cavalry's job on a wider scale and at a higher speed. Officially, therefore, the 12th was an armoured car regiment and the 13th/18th a tank regiment. So in spite of the fact that Derrick and his men were only in open carriers with Bren guns and we were in cars with turrets (these, too, were open to the sky – no lids to close down – but afforded *comparatively* greater protection laterally) we were to carry out our respective roles.

There was no cover on that road except for very young chestnut trees planted about fifty yards apart. Although we pressed our cars against them, once the Luftwaffe had found us they never left us alone. All the time we could hear the troops to either side of us reporting enemy. Some German motor-cyclists were on the move and when I checked the map reference I found that they were already behind me. There were the sounds of explosions to our rear, each of which sounded to me very like the bridge across which we were eventually to withdraw being sent sky-high.

Hours after the last of the '*braves Belges*' had retired through my position (at 60 m.p.h. and pointing back, shouting 'Les Allemands!! Un kilomètre par lá!!') no Allemands appeared. But eventually a posse of motorcycles came into sight some 600 yards distant. I was waiting until they came closer when Derrick's guns opened up with a roar that made me jump. The men and their machines just subsided in a heap in the middle of the road and lay there, some still astride their motorcycles.

For half an hour, I think about as bad a half-hour as ever I spent, I searched through my binoculars the road and the flat, grim countryside for their chums. But the whole treeless, unfenced, characterless, hideous wilderness was devoid of life. In front, Tirlemont with its nice people burned on in the hands of the enemy and explosions continued to rend the air from Louvain. I wished I knew what they were destroying back there. As an answer to my several reports, all I ever got from the operator back at HQ was a laconic: 'O.K. – off' (the equivalent to the Americans' 'Roger – out', which procedure we adopted later on). Perhaps it was comfortingly phlegmatic and when my turn came I am sure I sounded just as inhuman and unhelpful.

Then, at twelve noon precisely, Andrew Horsbrugh-Porter's voice came through the earphones. He told me to withdraw and come straight through Louvain to Beverloo. Relief outdoing shame, I informed Derrick as we passed through his carriers. He waved cheerfully and I never saw him again. It was 14 May and I had had five hours' sleep all told since Rowlands called me so long ago and in another world at Fonquevillers, (on 10 May.)

As we crossed the bridge at Louvain we all felt a lot happier for seeing the Guards there. They were the first British troops, bar Derrick's men, that we had yet seen. Furthermore they were, of course, cool, calm and collected. They looked at us without interest. They might have been waiting to line some royal route through London instead of a foreign river line shortly to be stormed by a relentless enemy which they knew to be vastly superior in numbers and armaments, if in nothing else. It was the first of many times during the next five years that we had occasion to be grateful for the Household Brigade.

Having made contact with the remainder of 'A' Squadron, Andrew led us to Ophern to 'rest'. No longer was I leading. It was just a case of following the car in front and maintaining correct intervals. I felt my map-case drop from my fingers. On reaching Ophern and seeing our troops settled, some of us were beginning to say things backwards and I found that people's outlines seemed to have white edges and misty haloes. By the time everything was squared up and the officers were at last able to sit down to some soup – in a very comfortable, clean, suburban house – heads began to crash forward. I do not remember going to bed. But what did eventually succeed in waking us was the shooting down at first light of a German plane directly over our house. We did not even bother to look out of the window, but went back to sleep at once. But our promised 'rest' was over, the pattern of things to come was established. We were ordered at once to Lennick St Quentin 'to guard General Gort'.

I noticed, en route, that map and country had little in common, though not yet as different as chalk from cheese, a situation we were to encounter later on. But we got there, and found our task different in practice from its relatively easy-sounding forecast. Having spent the entire night, when we could have been building up our tissues, watching a house to which a known fifth columnist was said to be returning 'any minute', he wisely refrained from putting in an appearance. So, at 5 a.m. (it was then 16 May) we moved to Braine le Château where we were given to understand that the Germans had already broken through at Waterloo. The 12th Lancers had been 'given the honour' of closing the gap. Some of us wondered, perhaps a mite sardonically, if the real reason was that there was no one else to do it.

For Bruce and I were given between us no less than six bridges to cover that night. While, therefore, there was still daylight, we set about blowing some of them up. It was not easy. To set the charges in the biggest bridge, a heroic sergeant of Royal Engineers had to swarm down one of our camouflage nets like a surprised lover leaving a bedroom window. As darkness fell we withdrew behind our already mined road-block, on the only road to Hal that the Germans could now use. This was to be blown in order to make even that road impassable, but only if or when we were sure we would not be using it again ourselves. The way things seemed to be going so far, we might as well have made a job of it there and then. We were agreeing to leapfrog back towards Hal as soon as the enemy came on, when we heard a certain amount of commotion near our bridge. Then the mine on the road went up unexpectedly and prematurely with a gigantic spout of flame, a red glow that lit the sky and a blast that knocked our hats crooked. A French officer in a staff car, accompanied by his French despatch rider, had set it off and, of course, been killed. But it had done very little damage to the road and we now heard the merry sound of approaching hoofs. A column of North African horse transport, about two miles long, came clip-clopping along to rattle unconcernedly over the 'crater'. They took half an hour to pass. The German tanks, we took mental note, would take considerably less than that. But these horsemen did not seem especially interested in us or the Germans, though one young officer, whom I stopped, took his pipe out of his mouth long enough to tell me that the latter were 'about seven kilometres way and advancing'. As they rumbled away I thought how Wellington's transport must have travelled that same road and at that same pace 125 years before. With the smell of sweating horse, fresh droppings and the fact that no one was talking they could have been the ghosts of Waterloo. After the last of them jogged off into the night and the nostalgic horse-aroma begun to fade, we strained ears and eyes towards the enemy, for though we had ammunition we had no more explosives. When it was certain that the enemy would be our next guests, our R.E. sergeant set off the charges in our bridge.

As dawn broke, the anti-tank guns of the Warwickshire Regiment were sent up to support us. We were delighted until told they were immediately leaving us again and that we were to cover their withdrawal! Throughout the morning we stayed on that river line while Hal was continuously dive-bombed to our immediate rear and the sound of bridges being blown *behind* us once again regularly split the air. Cows trotted past us along the middle of the road, mooing, milk squirting from their swinging and swollen udders. Angora rabbits skipped out of their way, wondering where to go. A lost dog ran by, ignoring us and the rabbits in its anxiety, too frightened to allow of kindness. It quickened its pace, tail down. A hastily abandoned house reminded one of a sort of dry-land *Marie Celeste*. An unfinished meal was still on the table, curtains fluttered out of the open windows, doors were unlocked and a fire was dying in the kitchen grate. It was civilisation on the run and I liked none of it.

I liked it even less when the situation dictated that Bruce's and my cars were the last Allied troops to cross the only remaining bridge to Hal. We finally went so fast that Bruce's hat blew off (a Herbert Johnson number from Bond Street – we were not wearing our tin hats). But 'the pace was too good to enquire' and he did not stop to retrieve it. Having had no sleep for thirty-seven hours, we expected to be given a night's repose on reaching Herrinnes. But at 3.30 a.m. it was back again to Hal to cover the further withdrawal of the infantry to the Dendre. By now German tanks were again shooting directly at us and as I came back round a corner at the rate of knots, I found my way blocked by a dense column of refugees. Not only that. My stationary car was gradually and firmly pushed sideways into the ditch onto its side by an enormous farm waggon full of people and their belongings.

We quickly got everything off the car, smashed the engine and I got onto yet another Morris to cover the final crossing, still with Bruce and some Lancashire Fusiliers at Deux les Acren. Again bridges were being blown behind us. Obviously they would be, but I never got used to it and, after one particularly large explosion immediately to our rear, I heard my squadron leader say, half to himself, 'This has just about cost us our lives.' But we eventually got over all right at a place called Buissenal.

Andrew Porter, John Erne, Bruce Shand, Andrew Roddick, Peter Arkwright, Henry de la Falaise and I slept that night on the kitchen floor of a tiny cottage. No mattress, pillow or blankets, just ourselves on a brick floor.

And I slept like a log. But at 3.30 a.m. in the now familiar dirty light of dawn we moved forward again to Lessines through an endless stream of retreating infantry, grey-faced with exhaustion. I made contact with the 4th/7th Dragoon Guards at Ostriches where Philip Verdin happened to have some tea ready and gave me a cup. I think that regiment lost most of a squadron on our right during that day.

There were masses of German infantry beyond the river where we had been the day before and a Gunner colonel, full of years, was bewailing the fact that he had not the guns 'to paste such a marvellous target'. 'Oh!' he cried, 'for just a couple of French seventy-fives!' 'And,' he added, 'where, oh where, is our Air Force?' Well might he ask, for it was another perfect summer's day – as regards weather anyway. Overhead and day after day German bombers flew unopposed, allowing their fighter escorts to come on down and strafe the living daylights out of anything and everything at treetop height.

That afternoon we passed through Tournai once again. The sunny town of flowering chestnuts and laughing girls with lilac sprigs was unrecognisable. Shops and homes were smouldering rubbish heaps. People and animals lay in the gutters either dead or bleeding to death. As we came to the main bridge, some idiot blew it up deafeningly in our faces, choking and blinding us with smoke and dust. The place had become a holocaust. We found a detour round the outskirts and got back to a place called Orchies where we enjoyed the very rare sight of three enemy bombers being shot down. Up till then the airbursts from our anti-aircraft batteries had always seemed to bloom well to the rear of any formation of bombers, in the unlikely event of their being engaged at all. 'Woompa-woompa-woompa' – and three little puffs of black smoke would appear in the sky, near the bombers but, like a moderate racehorse in *Raceform*, 'always behind'. The bombers would fly unswervingly on.

That night I slept till dawn in a large house with an extensive and pleasant orchard. Bersée proved the perfect place in which to hide all our cars until next morning, 20 May, when we were ordered to Arras, of all places. The Germans had already reached our recent 'homes', Fonquevillers, Hebuterne and Monchy. This was such startling news that we were not startled. Nothing was surprising any more. But all my kit was in an attic in Fonquevillers, including some very expensive best uniform . . .

En route our pace was seriously curtailed by hoards of refugees, cars bursting with passengers, mattresses on the roof, vast horse-drawn waggons all over the road carrying veritable households at about 4 m.p.h. It was incredible, therefore, that we moved all the way, to an area north of Avesnes (south west of Arras) across open plain, without being attacked from the air. But there were German tanks in Avesnes and, on contact with them, Sergeant

Knight (to be commissioned in the Desert) and Trooper Baker were wounded. The cheerful and efficient young Corporal Chambers was killed. We buried him there and then near Frevillers, where we took up positions beside the 1st Cuirassiers of the French D.L.M.

There followed one of those examples of sheer bovine stupidity that get men killed for no reason. My cars were in position and in observation of the enemy, when I noticed unusual movement immediately to my rear. It gradually sank in that my troop was being laboriously and painstakingly stalked by French infantry. They could see us watching them as easily as we could see them. It was difficult to comprehend. Our guns were all pointing in the opposite direction, we wore khaki, some of us wore British tin hats and we were making no effort to hide from them. As all our cars carried a Union Jack for recognition purposes, there came a moment when I decided it was time to show one. My gunner and I stood on the top of my car holding the flag spread out. 'Anglais!' we yelled. 'Nous sommes vos *amis*!' But neither my French nor my flag had any effect. They came stealthily along the ditch on their bellies, pushing their rifles before them. Had not Colonel Herbert at that moment driven up to and through them, accompanied by 'B' Squadron's French liaison officer, I cannot think how things would have turned out. The L.O. bravely ran down the road, waving his revolver, to meet them. He cursed the advance sections to their feet and screamed abuse at them. 'Yes,' he told me, 'they would have shot you dead. Les imbéciles! They had no officer.'

The same night we were recalled to Festubert. Andrew took me into his armoured car for the occasion, and while he slept on the floor at my feet, I led the squadron there through the moonlight with my torch lighting my map. By now we were in country so far back that we had not been expected to operate there. There were no one-inch maps. Mine was a 1918 quarter-inch, hopelessly out of date. I got there, occasionally having to dismount to shine my torch on a signpost, more by instinct than good map-reading, by practice, training and the feel of the thing.

There was a hot meal awaiting us in a house at Festubert and we were all more than ready for bed. But Colonel Herbert called in and sat with us while we ate, the very model of a live-wire commander, smart, clean, and radiating optimism. To our dismay, however, he ordered us, as soon as we had eaten, straight back whence we had come. As dawn was breaking we were back where we started. The situation round Arras had become too critical for rest. On the return from Festubert, Andrew Porter and I reversed roles. I slept on the floor while he read the map and I returned to my troop slightly refreshed. The French commander of the D.L.M. unit on my right strolled over to say good morning with a humorous expression on his face. He had some pork and hot coffee brought to me. But he said he was heartbroken. He had just been forced to abandon a pantechnicon containing 'two lovely pigs, a magnificent typewriter and a sewing-machine'. He had picked them up in some village 'just before the Hun got them'. I was sorry when the time soon came for us to part. We were ordered to Mont St Eloi.

During the whole of the war I never saw more enemy planes at one time than I saw that evening. They reminded me of starlings in November. Seeing that every single one of them was German we spent an unpalatable hour in a wood whence some of our tracers went close, though I never saw a hit. There was nearly always a Storch recce aircraft circling somewhere overhead. The pilot, as well as being brave, must have been fairly confident of air superiority, for we felt that even a Hurricane could have put paid to a Storch. But up till now the only British plane we had seen had indeed been a Hurricane, lying on some plough, quite whole but abandoned, near Huppaye which we passed on 12 May.

Now the Luftwaffe went home 'to change for dinner', as we put it, but our relief was short-lived. Orders came through that the 12th Lancers were to reconnoitre south towards Bapaume in an attempt to make contact with the French Army. The cold chicken that had been produced for supper turned to clay in at least one mouth. In tin cans of cars with only one third of an inch of armour plating, any attempt to get through country already in the hands of the German Panzers in order to *try to find* the French would obviously be suicidal. Even if we managed to by-pass the Germans, the 'Frogs' would let us have it!

Someone had found some quite good wine, which made the situation seem slightly less awful – or us more resigned. But I imagine we would have viewed our immediate future with disquiet even if we had been feeling properly rested and had lots of tanks and aircraft in support.

The counter-order which followed a few hours later ('The 12th Lancers will not operate tonight') was virtually a reprieve from a death sentence. We moved back to Bully Grenay where Bruce and I were allocated a very comfortable billet in the local doctor's modern house. When the doctor's wife saw us she just leant against the wall. 'Pauvres jeunes,' she whispered, 'quelle affaire!' She showed us to a roomy, carpeted bathroom in which we were to wallow in hot water and bath salts and shave in luxury.

Well before dawn we were on our way to Neuville St Vaast in preparation for reconnoitring forward from our former positions, held overnight by others, south from Frevillers. Having passed through the hamlet of Villers au Bois, we struck a sound grass track leading between hedges and with fields on either side. It was a nice morning and we had had baths and slept. I was thinking nevertheless how we would and should be better employed, such as riding horses on English grass. My car was third in line, behind Andrew's and John Erne's, another troop being well ahead of these HQ cars. There was not less than fifty yards between cars, single file.

I was stunned to see a Messerschmitt 109 more at hedge than tree height, coming straight at the leading armoured car. I then saw another plane go streaking over the second. Then, with an ear-piercing bang, my own car shuddered and filled with fumes as it was hit by yet another Messerschmitt's cannon. Each plane had singled out its own car. The last thing any of us lacked was perception and I always kept a wary eye on the sky. But none of us had seen this lot owing to their very low altitude, nor had we heard them because of the noise of our own engines. We accelerated into the hazel wood ahead of us, but the planes had already had time to circle round as we got into the covert, and were now coming in again in line astern, flying straight down the ride. One after the other they swept over us with howling engines, deafening gunfire and screeching tail winds. Everyone dismounted and took running headers into shellholes of 1914–18. But my wireless operator for that day, Sergeant Johnson, an intelligent, unflappable, pipe-smoking young Englishman stayed where he was, leaning against his set as if asleep; a cannon-shell had blown a hole you could put your fist through directly above him.

As we grovelled and, speaking for myself, prayed as never before, they came again and again. It was hell let loose and I do not think I ever again experienced anything quite so nasty or so noisy. When they had finished and we had crawled out of our blessed old shell-holes, shaken and covered in dirt, Andrew Porter had been hit in the hand, Trooper Jarret in the leg and Andrew Roddick's car put out of action. We managed to get Sergeant Johnson out of the car to lay him beside the ride. Peter Arkwright had been hit. He was somehow got to an ambulance train, but we were not to see him again. I remembered him so very recently after hunting in the snow, feeding the terriers at Hatton. We picked up Troopers Burns and Nutting (later to be my operator in the Desert and, after the war, to be commissioned in the regiment), who were walking from Peter's wrecked car. The Germans were firing from the next wood and when Bruce and I were dispatched to hold the high ground west of Vimy and the French infantry there began to pull out, I realised for the first time what chaotic conditions such warfare can impose.

Having not been to the Staff College, I wondered how any one man could ever have a truly accurate picture at such times. I tried to put myself among the High Ups. In calmer surroundings behind the line (what line?) and receiving continuous reports (who but us was continuously reporting?), I supposed they would be able to piece something together. I devoutly hoped so. But with everything happening so quickly, the situation so fluid and the German Panzers apparently going for the Channel ports regardless, it cannot have been easy. At least I now knew better what it must be like for the P.B.I. They could only know what their section or platoon was supposed to be doing. And in flame, smoke and general uproar that could hardly be other than difficult. So nowadays when I read critical biographies of generals, I feel that the authors might perhaps benefit from a 'baptism of fire'.

When the Germans crossed the Ridge, we were withdrawn, given new orders and sent forward again, this time to the mining village of Barlin. Fortunately for all, Colonel Herbert had 'a truly accurate picture'. As we drove out of this place, German bombers appeared to be engaged in formation drill, high above. They were showing off, and very impressive too. It was as if they had decided that, because they were winning so easily, it was not worth dropping any more bombs for the time being. Civilians were out in the streets in groups, staring at the sky. It was a lovely evening and they watched in some awe. It was certainly excellent enemy propaganda.

At last light we were once more recalled to Festubert where I slept till 3 a.m. At 3.45 a.m. I was on my way with my troop to Béthune. My task was to find out if reports that the enemy had occupied the place were true. I found it bombed to smithereens. Rubble, corpses, dead horses still in the shafts of overturned carts, ankle-deep broken glass everywhere, but no Germans. Six streets converged onto a sort of island signpost in the town centre. I was told to stay there covering these streets. It was a vile place in which to start a day and I was not disappointed when orders at last came through that I was to rejoin the rest of the squadron already on its way to St Omer. There were no reports that the Germans were already there. It was 23 May. I handed over thankfully to some carriers and got out of the town with the customary misplaced relief. Without knowing it, we were well and truly climbing out of the frying pan into the fire.

On reaching Ellinghem, en route for St Omer, other British troops assured us that 'Jerry was in the very next village'. But he was not. Instead we only found an isolated anti-aircraft battery who, not surprisingly, seemed extremely pleased to see us. For a big ugly brute of a German tank was breezing confidently along a parallel road. I noticed that it had a Nazi flag draped across it as aircraft recognition, scarlet and white in contrast to the bits of foliage that decorated our own vehicles in a touching attempt to camouflage them.

Another big black-looking tank came swanning along, with an enviable lack of caution, to join the first which had stopped. They were perhaps 400 yards away. I was willing them not to see us when Bruce started rat-tatting with his Bren, pouring tracer bullets into a wood occupied by enemy infantry on a bank the other side of the road from the tanks. The second tank traversed its gun so I loosed off at it with the Boyes rifle and hit it on the side of the turret. For all the effect it had I might have been a little girl trying to hurt a heavyweight boxer. It can only be by the grace of God that it did not retaliate. Perhaps its crew had not even noticed. I hit it a second time, as then suddenly rain began to come down as if someone had pulled a chain. Andrew told Bruce to observe the tanks and, perhaps luckily for him, also gave him a separate task. He then led the remainder of us up a side road, passing a British gun which had just been knocked out, its crew lying dead beside it. I saw a Heinkel weaving over us through the thick, low cloud and heavy rain, evidently intent on getting home. In fact it must have been thanks to the sudden, appalling weather that at least we had no further trouble from the air that day. But that could hardly have been much worse than what was on the menu instead.

When Andrew in the leading car stopped, Andrew Roddick brought his car up beside mine onto the grass verge. The rain was running in rivulets off his helmet. It was bucketing down.

'What the hell's happening, Tim?' he called.

'God knows' was my unhelpful but I suppose truthful reply.

Because the car in front moved on, we followed – and within seconds were right amongst German infantry. Our squadron leader acted swiftly and saved us from total destruction. He unhesitatingly swung off up a muddy track through a ploughed field yet to be sown. The track was not marked on the map and was as likely as not to be a dead end – in which case the term was likely to be appropriate as far as we were concerned.

The main lot of enemy infantry was lining the headland, in this case a shallow bank some fifty yards to our right. Some wore helmets, others were bare-headed. I got a quick impression of blond, sullen boys, pink-cheeked from the heavy rain. Their field-grey uniforms looked dark and sodden. They were either on all fours or flat on their stomachs. Bullets filled the air and I guessed most of them were ours for the enemy would scarcely have had time to collect themselves. A line of armoured cars coming round the corner must have been just as unpleasant for them as suddenly bumping into them had been for us. Now they were on three sides of us and all were being engaged. (There was, incidentally, no power-traverse to our turrets. It was therefore necessary to grasp the edges with both hands and pull the turret round manually, like an old-fashioned children's roundabout at a fair.)

The ruts grew deeper and muddier and the 15-cwt truck, which had somehow got itself betwen Andrew and me, stuck in front of me. To stick was to stop. Trooper Pearce, a Reservist, was my driver that day and I shouted to him to keep going. He could only do this by passing the bogged truck – and he did it. Unflustered by my yells and with admirable presence of mind, he swung the car out into the furrows and skidding and yawing, managed to regain the track successfully. It was a very good, cool piece of driving and the men off the truck scrambled aboard my slowly moving car as if they were catching a bus in the rush-hour.

I then saw that the dispatch riders, Owens and Cotton, had also stuck, coming to grief in the ruts on their motorcycles. 'Keep going!' I shouted. To stop now was to stop forever. Then Sergeant-Major Tree (now squadron sergeant-major, having been as good an officers' mess sergeant before the war as could be found), who was in my car, sank cursing to the floor, hit in the back of the neck. Somehow he continued to hand me up fresh magazines of ammunition for the Bren, which I was holding like a hose over the turret, off its mounting, to be able to change direction more quickly. I was firing from the armpit, tracers making aim unnecessary. Andrew was also standing upright in his turret in the car ahead, probably doing the same.

The Germans quickly recovered from their surprise and we now came under a heavy crossfire from small arms. No car got through without casualties. So it was a remarkable thing that mine should finish the course, as it were, with ten men in and on it and only Sergeant-Major Tree wounded. A bullet had scored a groove through the back of his neck, a nasty flesh wound, but he refused to go sick. Another bullet had holed my spare petrol tank. Otherwise car and occupants went unscathed.

It was now evident that the track ran on into a group of houses, unoccupied as yet by the enemy since the firing was lessening as we approached. So, as soon as we were on dead ground I dismounted and told Pearce to follow Andrew's car to the houses, but to wait for me there. I then ran back under cover of a bullfinch or high hedge away from the track to find the dispatch riders. I need not have bothered. I soon heard them coming, swearing (a good sign), whole and surprisingly happy. Together we ran to Linde where the rest of the squadron was now halted.

Nearing Linde, the dispatch riders and I were surprised to encounter a rocklike sergeant-major of Artillery, standing quite alone in the pouring rain, proud and smart in khaki greatcoat, webbing equipment, gas mask and tin hat. Being young, rather out of breath and more than fairly frightened, I enquired, probably as if he was very old and stone deaf, if he realised that the enemy was in the next field. His admirable reply: 'Thank you, sir, I heard the firing.'

The award of the DSO for this action to Andrew Horsbrugh-Porter said that he saved the guns which would otherwise have been captured. If the knocked-out gun we had passed early on was the right flank of this sergeant-major's battery position, then his guns would indeed have been captured but for 'A' Squadron, 12th Lancers. The Germans had just been heard to report 'enemy AFV activity' in this area.

Andrew told me to take the remaining cars to Hazebrouck while he went to report to the general there. I was thankful to find Bruce and his troop already ahead of us and when Andrew rejoined us from HQ, he led what was left of his squadron to Carvin. Here swarms of enemy bombers roared over, the rain having cleared away, but left us for another day.

I never sat down to a grimmer little supper with only Andrew and Bruce to share it. Both John Erne and Andrew Roddick had been killed. We slept till 1 a.m., but then had to stand to. It was a false alarm and we were able to lie down again until 4 a.m., but our rest had been broken.

At dawn we moved through Ypres to Roulers where the square was almost entirely covered with sleeping Belgian soldiers sprawled across the cobbles. Bruce and I, with just our two cars, were sent on to reconnoitre Ingelmunster. As we arrived, one of the ubiquitous Storch aircraft was circling the place and dropping the occasional flare, which we could hardly think auspicious. I rarely entered a place with greater trepidation. Scared Belgian infantry, prone in the roadside ditches just outside, completely ignored a wounded and bleeding civilian in the middle of the road. We took him out on the bonnet of one of our cars. He survived, but when we first saw him he was just being left to die.

Halfway through Ingelmunster we suddenly came under point-blank small arms fire. It is not as easy as one might think, chiefly owing to the din, initially to tell where it is coming from. But we agreed afterwards that it could only have come from top-storey windows either side of the street. Luckily it did not last. Our gunners raked the windows while our cars reversed at speed. By now Trooper Wessel had become my driver. A flamboyant character, he gave a yodel as he went into reverse. Like Pearce of the ploughed field, he kept his head and showed coolness and skill, turning the car and facing back to Roulers, while my guns never let up. We were now sitting ducks in the narrow street, but at least the firing from within Ingelmunster had ceased. Instead, we were attacked at low-level by Messerschmitt 109s. This time it was rooftop rather than treetop height, again and again, guns blazing. The noise alone almost stuns a man. As in the hazel wood, I got everyone out of the cars to huddle in a small cellar while I crouched on the floor of a tiny earth-closet. The planes howled along the line of the street, having it all their own way. Our cars were much holed and battered, but mobile, nor were there any casualties; so that when we were recalled to Wytschaete we were able to comply. Outside Ingelmunster, we met Peter Miller-Mundy and Andrew Henderson of 'B' Squadron, who had just had their dispatch rider killed and a car wrecked. Like every place that May, I was not sorry to leave it.

Before dawn, however, we were on our way to Neuve Eglise. We were to have been given a day's rest, but the regiment chosen to replace us had failed to turn up. So we were to spend the day determining the Belgian right flank and getting from them their dispositions, at the same time reporting on their condition. So, hearing that the Germans were 'through' north west of Ypres (through what?) Andrew sent me in my lone car to Poperinghe to confirm or otherwise. I had a jumpy sort of journey – I missed having a leading car more than I can say – but came upon a Belgian HQ at a place called Pilchem. Here I was shown a marked map by a very demoralised young Belgian ADC who spoke public-school English.

He was very angry that we should have offered help and then proved to have been 'of no help whatsoever'. When I replied that we were doing our best, he shouted at me 'No! No! Too late!' He said that there had been a tremendous lot of Belgian casualties at Poel Kappel (where our own RHQ had been the day before). He was an intelligent person and the utter futility of further resistance to 'this *juggernaut* of a German army' had got him right down. I was not thinking that way at all, but then my home was not in Belgium. On reporting over the air to Andrew, the latter sent me to Zonnebeeke, for the enemy were now said to have broken through 'somewhere there'. Again I was very glad to find that they had done no such thing. I reported this to Andrew who told me to go on to Dixmude. Here I encountered a cheerful officer of the 8th Cuirassiers, who appeared to be in full command of the local situation and was as refreshing to meet as the poor Belge had been depressing. So Andrew told me to come back to Ypres, where he posted me, in my car, under the Menin Gate itself, to watch the eastern approaches to the town.

The different attitude of our allies from that of our foe was here apparent. A little Belgian walked up to my car where I had an extensive field of fire and cover from air as well as being able to see a long way. He asked me if I would mind moving further away, 'if, that is, you intend to fire your guns.' There were, he explained, wounded men in the Cloth Hall and they needed quiet. Fortunately for all concerned I did not have to fire my guns, but I stayed where

I was until recalled. German cavalry were said to be swimming the canal to the north, but I had not seen anything.

Before leaving Ypres for Westyleteren I helped myself to a crate of champagne (quarter bottles) from the local wine merchants. The shops were open, but abandoned and deserted. There was a high-class confectioners opposite the Cloth Hall full of beautiful chocolates for the taking. It was a schoolboy's dream come true, but oddly enough, I had no sweet-toothed men in my troop. At Westyleteren we were shown to billets where we expected to be able to rest. But no. Once more we were woken appallingly early. But, having prepared to move out, we were then told we would be there 'for six more hours' . . .

It was 27 May and we had been continuously on the go for seventeen days with just a few hours' sleep, most, but by no means all, nights. So Bruce and I spent the morning asleep in the back seat of Andrew's Mercury staff car, which had strangely survived, driven by a trooper whom Andrew called Fred. As driver of that 'soft' vehicle throughout nearly three weeks of enemy air superiority, Fred must have had a nerve-racking time. We, in armoured cars, could keep an eye on the sky, but he could not. I am thankful to say that he came through unscathed.

The day was only remarkable for the fact that we did sleep undisturbed for five beautiful hours and that we actually saw with our own eyes a Hurricane fighter shoot down a German bomber. And that was remarkable because it was the only Allied aircraft we in 'A' Squadron had yet seen. We toasted the victorious pilot in champagne, which made us feel better. The Germans had started to drop leaflets with a map showing erroneously that we were encircled. We knew that we were not, but it may have affected some. 'British soldiers! Lay down your arms! Why go on fighting?' and so on. Nothing, of course, was more likely to spur British soldiers to fight to the death. (Three years later I was to remember these leaflets when we were dropping similar stuff on the Germans: 'Rommel beflohen!' for example, in Tunisia.)

We were still working on quarter-inch maps, vintage 1918, which were adequate out in the country, but divorced from reality in towns and suburbs. Early on 28 May Bruce and I were sent to observe and hold crossings over the Yser Canal, he at Schoorbakke, myself at Stuyvenskerke. I positioned the two cars allotted me (everything – men, cars, arms – was by now composite) under some Dutch barns, once again having cover from air and a perfect field of fire across the canal. The enemy, thinking to deliver the *coup de grâce*, drove up nose to tail to the main crossing on my right, held by Ned Mann ('C' Squadron) who surprised them in their over-confidence and won the DSO for his handling of the action. Sergeant Lewis was busy on my left.

What affected me personally was that my supporting Belgian infantry suddenly rose from the ground as one man and marched off in fours towards the enemy. This was so astonishing that I whipped up my car and sped to the head of the column to find out the cause of such rash behaviour. Quite simply and with a charming smile, their Commanding Officer informed me that the war was over. The Allies, he told me, were laying down their arms. 'We are going home,' he said. He spoke with relief as if saying 'Scheme over. Return to barracks, and thank the Lord for that!' I immediately reported on the R/T as I watched him go, a white flag now borne aloft at the head of his troops.

That the Belgians had capitulated was at once confirmed, but I had not known that when he first set off. One might have thought it would have an adverse effect on my soldiers. Quite the reverse. As usual, in adversity, extra witticisms broke out. An hour later just to add to the confusion, there was a very heavy thunderstorm during which my two cars were withdrawn and sent to help 'B' Squadron at Nieuport. From there we moved to Furnes, where we spent a beastly night patrolling the canal banks until the Sappers were able to destroy the bridges.

Bruce had been given a well-earned rest while Andrew took me, next day, to Bulskamp. Here we organised parties to carve a way through the multitude of abandoned Allied vehicles and equipment under an enemy-laden sky. During this difficult and irritating job, Colonel Herbert drove up in his staff car. He warned Andrew to 'expect another task'. In the meantime he was to take his squadron to Guyvelde.

Easier said than done. Unknown to any of us, the evacuation of Dunkirk had already started days before and those who had left for England, Home and Beauty had apparently just stepped out of their vehicles and gone. They might, we thought, at least have taken the trouble to pull in off the road, or, where impracticable owing to the wide and wet roadside ditches, at least as near the sides as they could get. Most were either in the centre or even at an angle *across* the road and anything not needed in the way of equipment had been dragged out of the backs of trucks and lorries, so that large piles of equipment and clothing were strewn knee-deep from verge to verge. As well as the trucks and lorries there were huge searchlights, many smashed and difficult to move. But many more were 100 per cent serviceable, having been driven as near to the coast as possible, meaning double-banking in a score of places, before what must, by all the signs, have been a fairly panic-stricken departure.

We liked to think it was perfectly normal that the depleted 12th Lancers should still be operating smoothly amidst this chaos. 'Another task' was not forthcoming and when we had got back to the last canal we received the order to save the arms but destroy the four remaining armoured cars. The Boyes Rifle was fired at point-blank range into the engines and they were then heaved over backwards to sink in the canal. They were no great loss. What did hurt was watching the D.L.M. doing likewise with their Panhards, so infinitely superior to our Morrises. The flat, low-lying terrain was now being purposely flooded, and the fields to either side of the ruler-straight roads were beginning to fill. A French horsed regiment had turned its horses loose. We thought they might have taken the trouble to remove the saddles and bridles, but no. Wandering in the rising flood and appearing on the whole to be content grazing here and there along the banks, were many horses still saddled and bridled with broken, trailing reins.

Andrew sent me back 'to find the transport'. I do not think I had, or have ever, been given a more apparently impossible job. Someone had to do it, to be sure, but without car or wireless it was on a parallel with being told by a racegoer in the Epsom stands on a fine Derby Day to go across the course and find his pet kitten. Amidst all the copious and widespread litter of defeat and surging hordes of khaki-clad men reaching back as far as the eye could see, I just wished that he had not chosen me.

I caught hold of a horse, felt for the girths and mounted. Then I started to ride back through the wreckage of an army and a milling mass of retreating men. My horse wore an officer's saddle. He was a grey with quite a bit of quality, had obviously been well ridden and was as quiet as a sheep without being a slug. It was just a case of threading our way, sometimes through floods – I could not use the only road – and keeping my eyes and ears open. I had not ridden much more than a mile when, to my indescribable surprise and relief – and Andrew's too, I dare say – I saw a familiar face. I had found the transport.

What a dear good horse! Riding back to Guyvelde I had to push through crowds like a mounted policeman at a Cup Final. The air was full of tracer, and anti-aircraft guns were going strong. Just to see and hear them was wonderful and my good horse ignored the noisy pandemonium. Men who had had no apparent protection from the Luftwaffe for three whole weeks, were standing there in the open, shaking their fists and yelling abuse at the enemy planes. Not that it did any harm to the Luftwaffe, but it did relieve the pent-up frustration of the much-strafed. To us it was nothing less than a miracle to see anyone besides ourselves still in the match, as it were.

When at last I got back to squadron headquarters I had to say farewell to my horse. I then led the way on foot (Andrew took the horse) to the transport so that the now dismounted squadron could gather for a hot evening meal. Someone had recovered a terrified terrier pup from inside a ditched truck and was sharing his food with it. 'There must', observed its rescuer, 'be some right bastards on their way home, if they are not already there.' When we had finished, everything was either burned or destroyed, but the regiment was still together and fully armed.

Next morning, 30 May, when the regiment marched on foot to La Panne to embark on waiting ships, Bruce and I carried a Boyes Rifle each. Halfway along the barrels was slung a box of ammunition. Troopers Hallsworth and Brayshaw were amongst those who took turns to carry the other ends. Dismounted cavalry become 'weak infantry' and one way and another by the time we reached our goal, if not long before, I certainly fitted that description. But there, indeed, were the little ships standing close inshore. We were as good as home. Or were we?

One man, it was now discovered, was without the Bren with which he had started. Hearing of this, Colonel Herbert personally ordered him back, alone, towards the advancing enemy with orders not to rejoin the regiment without the gun. He returned, carrying it, four hours later. Now instead of embarking as expected, we were told that we would 'police the beach for twenty-four hours'. That as may be imagined, put a rather different complexion on things. When every minute counted, twenty-four hours sounded like a life time – or a death sentence. I have since heard that 'those in the know' lost hope at this juncture, and indeed at this time, I was told in all sincerity by an intelligent and successful businessman – a temporary 12th Lancer officer and a good one too – 'I suppose you realise this means surrendering the Royal Navy?' I certainly didn't and crossly said as much. For me (and all the other regular soldiers by the look of them) defeat was both impossible and unthinkable and that kept us reasonably happy. And the reason we felt as we did was due to nothing else but upbringing and training: the training, laughed at, not to say derided today, of home, school, Sandhurst and the regiment, or, in my own case, two regiments.

We started at once on our new task. We drove all the lorries we could muster into the sea at low tide. Head to tail they formed piers when the tide rose. We personally rowed the soldiers of other units out to the ships and brought the empty boats back for more. I did that twice only – two times too often. On my second trip I called (having disgorged my passengers and therefore in an empty boat except for another 12th Lancer who did his best to keep the thing steady) alongside a destroyer. I politely enquired if a sailor or two could be spared to help. I was equally politely but a shade reprovingly told: 'The ship's officers are at dinner, sir'. Even under those circumstances I thought that, like the Royal Artillery sergeant-major's near Linde, that was at least an admirably British reply. I was incredulous and probably grinning with rage, yet it made me feel that, perhaps, things were not as bad as they seemed. To a couple of soldiers bobbing up and down in rather a large rowing boat in deep water with the light going, they couldn't have. Anyway, as we rowed an erratic course back to the khaki queues ashore, I hoped, how fervently I hoped, that the officers' port (or pink gin) choked them.

It did little to improve morale next morning to see one of their perfectly sound boats lying capsized when the tide receded. We righted it and put it to use. But I got invaluable help from a naval officer, Godman by name, a school contemporary, who was everywhere at once, capless and bare-footed, clad only in grey flannel slacks and a monkey jacket. From a post war Old Stoic list I discovered he had been killed in the war and won the DSC. If the DSC was for what he did at Dunkirk, he deserved it several times over.

At last the hour came when the 12th Lancers formed up to march seven miles along the beach towards Dunkirk itself. Seven miles sounds far enough for 'weak infantry'. Hope made the march a mere nothing. We were only attacked from the air once, so we rightly assumed that the RAF must be somewhere even though we still had not actually seen a representative. On this occasion we scattered into the dunes and poor Trooper Bloom was hit. He had to be left at a casualty clearing station. But he was all right because I met him after the war in 1948 when the regiment was at Colchester. He was then running his own business somewhere on the East Coast.

Halfway along the beach we looked back at La Panne and watched our recent area being blotted out by heavy shellfire. Then Colonel Herbert came to meet us in his shooting brake staff car. He smilingly informed us that he had made arrangements for our departure and when our turn came we just waded out to the waiting boats. My nearest neighbour at the time was Henry de la Falaise.* As the water rose coldly to our chests, I noticed a bundle on his head, some belongings wrapped in a gas cape. He noticed that I was looking at them. 'My divorce papers!' he explained with a laugh. He survived to write a book (*Through Hell to Dunkirk*, published in America). Clothes heavy with water, I clambered into a life boat but, as it became overcrowded, the officers were told to get back into the sea. There were trailing ropes to clutch. We clutched.

*The Marquis de la Falaise, a gallant veteran of the First World War, had been posted to 'A' Squadron, 12th Lancers, as an *agent de liaison* early in 1940 and he was of enormous assistance during the campaign. In his youth he had led a somewhat stormy life in Hollywood, marrying in succession Gloria Swanson and Constance Bennett. The 'divorce papers' mentioned here refer to the latter lady.

5
Into the Desert

The 12th Lancers made a somewhat uncomfortable and disorganised voyage – fortunately free of air-attacks – in a diversity of vessels, from Dunkirk to Margate, to land on the morning of 1 June. After a week or so everyone was miraculously reunited at Hamworthy, near Poole, in Dorset. Within a short time the regiment was re-equipped with highly dangerous vehicles, called Beaverettes, nothing else being available.

A move to East Anglia, to repel the expected invasion, found Tim still with 'A' Squadron, and, as ever, he managed to go racing and later to get some hunting with the Crawley and Horsham, when a further move was made to Sussex.

Inevitably there were changes after the disastrous three weeks' campaign. Familiar faces disappeared – especially when the 27th Lancers were formed – and he was not the only one who found himself unhappy with a new régime, about which his diary makes trenchant criticism.

However, matters eventually improved with the arrival of new Humber armoured cars, and 'A' Squadron was now commanded by Rodney Palmer, to whom he was much attached. Most of the summer of 1941 – probably the most calamitous year of the war – was spent under canvas on Salisbury Plain, before a final move to Westbury, prior to embarkation at Avonmouth for the Middle East.

There ensued a placid six weeks on a very well-found ship, Highland Brigade, through the Atlantic. Like most of its passengers, Tim enjoyed this trip, which provided ample time for reading, and he records that he finished War and Peace. At Durban there was transhipment to a vast Dutch liner, after a somewhat riotous week ashore, tragically marred by the accidental death of Maurice Barker.

A swift rush up the coast of East Africa to Aden, and then through the Red Sea, brought the regiment to Port Tewfik, where he was appointed 'baggage master' – I think he gave himself this somewhat archaic title – and had an enjoyably independent time bringing, by rail, all the impedimenta, intact, to a very stark camp at Amiriya, to the west of Alexandria, where he received the sad news of his father's death.

By early December the 12th Lancers were in the Desert under the com-
mand of 7th Armoured Division, engaged in the pursuit of the enemy, who
were making a fighting withdrawal to the south west. Tim was now second-
in-command to Rodney Palmer.

The 12th had already been ordered to patrol south of the impending battle,
from a place called Um Ed Dragg. Such 'places' were rarely more than map
references. There might be a well or, more likely, just a cairn, but featureless
desert was what one usually found. This battle resulted in a defeat for the
enemy, who began their retreat to Agedadia. For the next three days,
therefore, we were constantly on the move, often crawling and bumping
over going only fit for a goat, in a wind so cold that overcoats, gloves and
balaclava helmets were the fashion. We were much bothered by a single
Messerschmitt 110 that liked to fly low over my car, machine-gunning as it
went. After taking a dose of tracer from my Bren it kept off for the rest of
the day. But an Italian plane, to which my driver referred as 'that Al Capone
two-stroke', while never venturing within shot, kept circling us in a
tiresomely inquisitive manner. Next day, during a halt, he suddenly appeared from behind a rise flying exceptionally low and right over us. He
must have been as surprised as we were. But I hosed him with tracer and
Bruce, who was standing out in the open, mug in hand, cried, 'You've got
him, you've got him!', and though he did not waver in his flight we never
saw him again.

Next morning we reached Msus, a fort so recently vacated by the Italians
that a fire was still burning and Bruce reported with distaste that their beds
were still warm. There were papers that were important, a splendid and
much-decorated uniform jacket or two and one steel helmet with the name
'Luigi' written inside. Rodney Palmer told Bruce to take everything to RHQ.
'Right,' said Bruce, 'but I'm damned if I'll carry Luigi's hat!'

Later a ME 110 appeared and settled in to give us stick. It would fly away,
then come banking round for a long run in, machine gunning as it came. Its
pilot was quite fearless, and probably angry enough to get careless – which
is why we thought it must be the same plane we had managed to hit earlier
that week. He ignored our Bren, but singled out my car for his second run.
He started machine gunning from about a mile away on his return journey,
at first a sound rather like Masefield's 'tearing sacking' but soon the old
familiar uproar of engine and guns combined, so bad for morale on the
receiving end. He did not hit us nor, apparently, we him, so he gave us a
repeat performance. This time I slipped down inside the turret and, when
the cross-wires were on his nose, gave him four rounds of the big Besa. He

howled overhead, leaving us with our customary rocking-cum-deafened sensation and vanished. Silence.

'Have you by any chance just shot down a Messerschmitt 110?' The commanding officer (Peter Burne) himself was on the air. 'One has crashed more or less at my feet!'

The pilot and his gunner were brought to squadron headquarters, where we gave them cigarettes and sent them back to the nearest casualty clearing station, the pilot's face being particularly badly cut. The shooting down of this plane was reported on the London BBC News on Christmas Eve 1941. Charles Morrison-Bell was quick to snaffle the brandy off the crashed aircraft.

Early next morning, during an attack directly on 'A' Squadron by the Luftwaffe, I had my precious sun compass shot right away and received four hits on my turret, one chipping its edge, and six more on the car's rump. The transmission was damaged by bomb splinters and one of the shock-absorbers similarly sliced. Three good men, who had been eating breakfast beside their truck, dived under it, but were killed. Near at hand, Alan Carson lost three men wounded, including Owen (who survived the war). Immediately after which twenty-six Hurricanes of the RAF came weaving over, slowly circled us and flew away east. We thought their minds were more on their pre-luncheon gin and tonic, but at least we had actually seen Allied aircraft.

Christmas Day was dreary, very cold and overcast as the regiment moved to Saunnu. This was a slight hollow with a 'well with wind-pump', as the maps had it. Here were also the Royals, the Gloucester Hussars and the County of London Yeomanry. But there was little time to intermingle before moving out to leaguer, the whole regiment together for that night. The Tobruk water that we were now getting was slightly saline so my only Christmas present was very welcome: SSM Knight still had some good water on his car and filled my empty flask. 'This would go well in the next Journal,' he suggested. 'Which officer filled his flask with *water* on Christmas Day?'

'No one would guess,' I said.

Rodney Palmer had got a box of cigars which he generously circulated until it was empty. Peace and goodwill held temporary sway. Temporary. For 28 December was a black day. My squadron was in reserve with Brigade HQ at Chor es Sufan and was unsuccessfully dive-bombed after lunch. As the Stukas flew away with that rather unsteady, gorged-vulture look about them, a shower of brilliant green recognition flares rose into the air from a distant column to the north of us. The Stukas did not deviate, but flew on over the column, leaving us in no doubt whatsoever that it was German. Considering this was headquarters with, to quote my diary, 'generals and things here and there', there appeared to be alarmingly little concern. Eventually Charles Gregson was sent by the General to 'go and have a look'. Having to advance across open desert he was, of course, immediately shelled. But it was not until one or two of these shells started plopping into Brigade HQ itself, setting a lorry on fire, that any sort of a move was made. It was then too late for many.

The column was now east of us and travelling south at a fair pace. There were at least 26 tanks and reportedly, 150 anti-tank guns, and they were sending across air-bursts to the west of us. Temporarily and disconcertingly, we got the impression of being gradually surrounded. There could be only one sensible thing to do – try to escape the net by going in the same direction as the enemy, parallel with them, but faster. By now they were shelling like old Harry and British lorries were careering hither and yon, getting stuck or bursting into flames. When Rowly Beech's armoured car got stuck the enemy were only 300 yards away and closing in, using Tommy guns. Rowly was picked up, but I saw the lorry, which had most of my better kit on it, stick and the crew leap onto passing armoured cars. I had lost my clothes in France and this looked like more expense, though that hardly mattered when lives were at stake. Wilson sent the Humber along like a bolt from the blue and it was with a feeling of incalculable relief that I saw the head of the German column halt, turn west and start off again moving across behind us.

There followed a peaceful night, but next morning 'C' Squadron was caught by dive-bombers. For once, owing to the direction of the wind, I never heard these planes and nor did 'C' Squadron just the other side of the ridge. The first thing that any of us knew was that bombs were bursting all over the place, one of which killed Trooper Curly, who had been my gunner on the squadron's pre-war trip to Penzance. Three other men died and the SSM was wounded. There was a new mood of anger, as though we had been stabbed in the back. But an enemy column was approaching fast from the west and we were told to 'determine its tail'.

We had therefore to drive westwards along the ridge on its northern flank, an unattractive job since we were shelled all the time. In spite of our reports – I suppose again because we were new boys – the General, now out of range and presumably earshot, was allegedly wondering whether this might not be 'a lost South African column returning from yesterday's holocaust'. It was one of those days when one lost all sense of time as one peered endlessly through one's binoculars, reporting back and trying to keep out of trouble. Our reports were at least believed when the column got to Haseiat and anybody who poked his nose into the place got it accurately shelled on the instant.

That night was a most uneasy affair. The strong enemy column had taken possession of Haseiat and there was a continuous rumble of tanks and vehicles moving through the darkness and a near-continuous display of Verey lights as they gathered in their strays. It was a show of strength too. I thought it more than likely that we would find ourselves encircled by first light, but this the enemy had not even attempted. Instead, as dawn broke, forth they came *en masse*. Due north, straight at us, an imposing forest of vehicles, many shelling as they advanced. They looked uncommonly invincible and I personally found the order to withdraw extremely welcome. The battle, we were assured, was 'going according to plan'. But it had hardly started and we had heard that one before. In France we had withdrawn according to plan until we were aboard a Thames dredger heading for Ramsgate. This time, however, there was a sudden counter-banging from the guns of our friends in tanks over the ridge. Very brave men, and I was glad to be in an armoured car instead of having to slog it out with armour-piercing and high explosive shells. But the enemy got what he wanted – time. Time to get his main forces away round the corner from Agedabia before himself withdrawing. To my eye, he had looked as if he could have gone to Benghazi. But that was not his plan. He wanted to form a fresh line behind which he could build up his diminished strength. For our part we were told that the idea was to 'contain the enemy for two months and then destroy him'. But, we told each other, that was giving the opposition exactly what he wanted – time to get his strength back and destroy *us*. That he was damnably good at his job had not escaped us.

Even as soon as 6 January 1942, in a sandstorm that reduced visibility to twenty yards, our patrols were pushed west again. Another distasteful task, since, when last seen the previous day, the ground to be made good had been covered with enemy vehicles. However, after advancing into the murk some eleven miles without incident, we were able to confirm that he had indeed departed. Johnny Henderson showed noticeable daring in penetrating the thick veils of blowing sand, once coming suddenly face to face with a German tank, a nasty moment until it was found to be an abandoned victim of that earlier clash. Even so, the fact had to be established, and more quickly than might have been considered healthy in the need to push on. But again our reports were doubted, our advance unexploited and we were recalled 'to rest for forty-eight hours'. Rest? The very next morning we received the message: 'Enemy withdrawn. Prepare to move at 1500 hours.' Having spent the whole of the previous day risking life and limb across through appalling going and pea-soup visibility in order accurately to report this very fact, none of us felt inclined to cheer.

Throughout this period the cold was considerable and our appetites correspondingly sharp. I actually liked Fray Bentos, but there were those unfortunates to whom cold bully was anathema. On 11 January, after a two-day struggle across soft sand, we found ourselves in the weird landscape of the Burruei Basin. By then we were some eighty miles' difficult going in advance of our transport. Rations and water became short, and, during the ensuing eight or nine days, I have never been so hungry or thirsty in my life.

Apart from the shooting up and capture of a German armoured car by Johnny Henderson and George Yates, we mostly sat and observed the stationary foe – with hunger gnawing our vitals and thirst beginning to nag. We were frequently worried and, in my case, frightened stiff by Stukas. They burned both our squadron supply lorries and their escorting ME 109s spattered us with bullets and cannon during one particularly unpleasant and prolonged afternoon attack. My car was hit seventeen times, but nothing came through. When it was all over, the mail truck managed to reach us and my first letters, three airgraphs from Molly, were handed up to me.

The soft sand had played havoc with the cars and fitters performed miracles in keeping them going. Our cars had been constantly on the go for five weeks and the extra and quite out of the ordinary effort to get through such going was killing them one by one. We had seventeen left of our sixty-three starters. In fact Rod [Rodney Palmer] in the forward link and I in the rear link to RHQ were now carrying out patrols as a troop. To give some idea of the conditions, as the only local well was salty we finally drained the fresh water out of our cars' radiators and replaced it with well water. The radiator water was rust red and had a distinctly metallic flavour, but it did make drinkable tea. One evening I gave Peter Willes a lift back to leaguer for the night, his car having finally packed up. My own car began to overheat owing to the ground we were grinding across and started to lose power. Peter commented on the overheating and I was able to explain, to his considerable surprise, that we'd drunk the water out of it.

It was as physically uncomfortable a period as we had yet known. The icy wind sought us out as we crouched in our comfortless turrets full of hard, sharp edges and projections. A mournful wind whined and occasionally screeched shrilly across the salt-marsh, the ultimate in desolation. Sometimes it picked up the sand and flung it, mixed with cold rain, in our faces. We wore our anti-gas goggles, but there was no place where sand did not penetrate. But it was a choice of evils: if the weather cleared, it made way for the Luftwaffe. Besides, I never doubted that it was five-star comfort compared with the trench warfare of the 1914–18 winters.

On 20 January we were at last taken out of the line. We were recalled to Msus 'to rest and refit'. That, at least, was the good intention. In fact the Germans began their advance the moment they saw us go. They were on us in five days, having virtually swanned through the unfortunates who had relieved us. On our way back to Msus we had noticed, more with surprise than dismay, the lack of anything that could fight. We passed through acres of ACVs, tents, lorries, divisional signposts and military police. But there was hardly a tank or a gun to be seen. We now heard that shortage of petrol was hampering the activities of the Bays, the 9th Lancers and the 10th Hussars (2nd Armoured Brigade).

On 25 January we finished washing ourselves and our clothes (in half petrol tins of saline water) and spread our clothes to dry over the camel scrub. We were revelling, too, in a proper shave. We were not, therefore, pleased to be suddenly smothered in dust by a vast horde of desperately driven vehicles pouring back towards the east. We paused in our ablutions and those who had been sunbathing sat up. The sound of machine guns firing in our direction seemed strangely and uncomfortably local. One hundred and thirty enemy tanks were said to be moving up from Saunnu. Are the 12th Royal Lancers the only people in this war who can deal with the turbulent Hun?' we asked each other, as we snatched our still wet shirts and pants from local scrub and flung them into blanket boxes. The order to move out came in the nick of time, but my dear old car had had enough. She refused to start. 'Oy-oy-oy-oy-oy-oy-oy-oy-grunt!' went the self-starter. 'Oy-oy-oy-grunt!' Then: 'Oyoyoy oyoyoyoyoyoy- 'She won't have it, sir!' called the totally undismayed Wilson from the driver's seat.

WOOMF came the first German shellburst and again WOOMF, right slap into our rest area. Then flame spouted from the lorry on our left, the far side of the track. Black smoke began to billow across. Feeling that our last hour had really come this time, we jumped from our reluctant armoured car and hailed a lorry. Its driver and Wilson fixed a towrope onto the armoured car with the speed of light, and away they went together, bumping and swaying at speed across the desert sand. Rod reached down from his turret as he came up the track, hauled me up onto his car and I sat at his feet beside his grinning operator. Crouched there listening to Rod collecting the squadron as at Aldershot, I had an incongruously cosy feeling; in spite of the time, place and conditions, I was happy. We drove to Charruba where we stayed the night. After ten miles of being towed flat out, Wilson reported to me that 'the old brute had decided to start'. She finished the course without her tow. 'But', Wilson added, worried for once, 'she's wrong of her wind somewhere, sir. Definitely.'

After we had retreated as far back as Mechili, the fact must have been grasped by the authorities that the 12th Lancers just had not enough cars to continue operationally. Therefore those that were still mobile were handed over to Bruce to form a small composite squadron. The rest of us were ordered to El Adem.

6
Retreat

We moved into leaguer near El Adem airfield on the last day of January 1942. 'It was', says my diary, 'the blackest, barest, characterless and most withered mudflat yet seen'; which, after Burruei, was saying a lot. But for the first time we slept safe in the knowledge that, however fast the enemy came on, they could not possibly reach us until well into the next day. Who else besides Bruce was supposed to be barring their way was anyone's guess. Nor is it clear in the history books. But by 4 February a line was held from Gazala to Hacheim. It was a wonderful thing to hear music again. As soon as our sets were switched off officially, I asked Downton to try to get some music. Presently I heard *Meditation* by Massenet coming sweetly over the air. Ever after, it has taken me back into the desert just as Wagner still reminds me of grooming black horses in the yard at Windsor.

We now moved further back to railhead. Again it was open, flat and stony desert, but it was away from battle, we slept in pyjamas, ate in a mess tent sitting at a table and drank out of glasses. And when 'A' Squadron beat RHQ at football one Saturday afternoon, it *felt* like Saturday instead of the days and nights all one long watch-and-report, split up by light and darkness. The weather was perfect, the company always good. I noticed Neil [Speke] had two empty gin bottles, necks downwards in the sand, planted either side of his bivouac entrance. 'While I'm here, I'm going to drink myself a garden fence', he explained. Obviously there were low points. I did not, for instance, greatly care for Reveillé. The colonel had decreed that the regiment should be called each morning by a burst of Bren gun fire. It was a rude, though effective, awakening.

On 18 February I took a detachment the 400 miles to Cairo. My mission was to bring back new armoured cars. Leaving early, we reached Daba by nightfall and Cairo in the middle of the following afternoon. That night, at Shepheard's, I ran three consecutive baths, two to wash, the third to rinse. I had a bottle of Krug in an ice-bucket on a chair beside the bath. And as good luck would have it, the cars were not ready for us. So we went racing at Gezira on Saturday and at Heliopolis on Sunday, and met so many friends and saw so many familiar faces that I wondered what proportion of the Army had been left to defend Britain. After a week we started back up the desert. The first night we spent in the transit camp at Amiriya and heard Winston Churchill on the radio telling us we could win. What had a magic effect on morale was the way he ended: 'But westward, look, the land is bright!' The sound of his voice was a tonic anyway; and in spite of all, we somehow knew we should eventually win.

I slept the next night in a wadi, already bright with little spring flowers, outside Mersa Matru. There were miniature dandelions, cornflowers, 'carriage and pair', tiny mauve orchids and – my favourite, because the scent brought back so vividly the New Forest garden of my childhood – marigolds. Also the smell of crushed grass, as we drove out over the little green patches, was uplifting after so much sand. Refreshed after my unexpected spell of leave and sitting on the top of the turret as we sped along through a pearl of a morning, the sea very near on our right, my heart was singing. But after turning off and leaving the calm blue of the Mediterranean behind, gales and sandstorms soon hit us. My songs ceased, I got down inside the car and we had a rough time reaching the regiment. As soon as I decently could, I made a beeline for the small mess tent, which looked as if it might take off any moment. Inside and alone sat Peter Willes trying to write a letter through a layer of sand on a flapping piece of paper.

'Welcome home,' he said.

Trying out the guns next day, the 7.92 on my car kept firing one shot then jamming. 'It's these bloody women they have in the factories now, sir,' said Wilson. 'Why don't they stick to making pies?' On 3 March, with all in working order, we moved forward again, leaguering near 'The Wire' in deluging rain. We were all soaked through and, before dressing in the morning, I first emptied the water out of my desert boots and wrung out my socks – though, since the water was ankle-deep, I need hardly have bothered. I splashed across to breakfast, a standing affair beside the officers' mess truck, which would stay with us until we went back into the line. Rod held out a steaming mug of tea. Being accustomed to pour my own, I was surprised until I took a sip and found it was half whisky, not perhaps to be recommended as a regular breakfast dish, but on this occasion a saver.

One remembers these little acts of kindness. Another was on our first night back in line. I was already lying on my bed when it started to rain. Suddenly a tarpaulin off the car landed on top of me, thrown over me like a New Zealand rug by the ever-considerate Wilson.

On 12 March Rod had to go off on an exercise and I had my first taste of commanding a squadron in action. So that had to be the day that fifty enemy vehicles, preceded by tanks, decided to come swanning into our sector, leaving us no option but to fall back before them. Like the Duke of Plaza Toro, I led my squadron from behind until the enemy halted. A reconnaissance in force? For they later turned round and we were back in the same position when Rod arrived with three Senussi agents perched like white Wyandottes on his armoured car. I was very pleased to see him.

The enemy economised in reconnaissance units by employing a ME 110 and two ME 109s – or so it seemed to those of us who saw them every day, wherever we might be, flying unmolested directly over us. They came so regularly that you could nearly set your watch by them. I never did see them tackled.

On 20 March I again took over from Rod, who had to go and see General Herbert Lumsden. After he had gone, I was hoping for a nice uneventful day or two when the commanding officer came on the air in person. He wanted me 'to find out if the enemy O.P. was still on the hill called Eleba.' The latter completely dominated our squadron front. On this particular occasion, it was, needless to say, not only blanketed by low cloud, but partly hidden by a ground mist as well.

Out of this fog the enemy suddenly once again appeared, making straight for us. It so happened that, by a miracle, I had at my disposal some 25-pounders and these I was able to employ without any delay and the tanks were stopped in their tracks. At the same time, I heard over the air 'B' Squadron on my left reporting 'a mass of enemy stuff' at Mechili. 'They are in *close* leaguer, there are two more hours of daylight. Can't *someone* come and bomb them?' All that happened was that a small force of German bombers, escorted by a lot of Italian fighters, arrived just before dark to bomb 'B' squadron. By the grace of God, there were no casualties.

On top of this, George Yates and Sergeant Arrowsmith were sent to 'lay out ground signals to guide the RAF to Mechili'. This entailed their getting uncomfortably close to the place. And the result of their efforts? 'The desert sand took a fearful hammering,' said Arrowsmith. The 'invisible men' – as we then called the RAF – had arrived to drop their lot on nothing.

But the invisible men were no such thing on the day that six of their Bostons bombed RHQ in the Teilim Hills, killing a 12th Lancer. They later sent some poor chap to fly over the place and dip in salute as apology, alone and unescorted. Everyone prayed he would return to base untroubled by the vicious and ubiquitous 109s.

It was then that 'A' Squadron was chosen to escort a column which was to probe some thirty miles behind enemy lines (Mechili-Tmimi) in order to shell the Martuba landing ground. This meant by-passing the enemy-held Eleba after dark, leaving their flares whooshing up uncomfortably to our rear. All next day we maintained a protecting screen for the column – from the ground. Otherwise they were continuously attacked from the air for six and a half hours. While the Stukas were away filling up their bays with more bombs, the 109s kept the pot boiling. Their organisation was faultless and it went on all day long with such a frightening intensity that I was, as always, thankful to hear the words 'Withdraw. Mission accomplished.' Simultaneously with this order, three British bombers with no less than twenty-two fighters arrived overhead in the empty evening sky. But the Hun had gone. Next day the BBC reported: 'A successful raid was carried out by highly mobile units including armoured cars.' Fair enough. But: 'Sandstorms prevented our planes taking off to give air support.' As 'A' Squadron went speeding back through the enemy lines, single file through the night, I looked back and saw the wireless aerials and their fluttering recognition pennants and thought, as I so often did, how like our forebears' lances they looked silhouetted against the moonlit dust. But how much better in 1942 to be in an armoured car.

Next morning we took up our same line of observation. To give some idea of the front we 'observed', when Rod and I visited the troop positions we covered eighty miles. Once we stopped so that the squadron leader might photograph the nest of a buzzard, or desert turkey. We had seen the bird flouncing off through the camel-scrub at our approach and found her two eggs, one of which was in the process of hatching. We also found a tortoise and kept it until our next move; then we left it amongst the wild flowers, having written 'Mark IV' on its shell in large black figures. If the Germans found it, they would look upon it as an ally. I often wondered if they did.

On April Fools' Day we left our familiar haunts amongst the patches of wild flowers and moved south, away from the sea. Our new sector was made up of the stony, airless and dusty wastes about Bir Tengeder and there were vast tracts of desert as brown as ploughed fields and about as interesting. While we were en route to take over from the Royals, three Italian fighters flew over, Macchi 202s, most unexpectedly since they came directly from the south. They turned and, keeping well wide of us, circled ominously, having a good look. We awaited an attack, but they flew away to the north and we completed our journey in peace.

We found Tony Barne's squadron HQ amongst some rocks at the base of a small escarpment. 'You've arrived just right for a gin and lime,' he greeted us, welcome words when we were all 'spitting sixpences' after sixty dust-blown miles. It's quiet down here,' he said. 'You'll be bored stiff.'

But Good Friday came two days after his departure and with it twelve Italian Macchi 202 fighters, possibly the same ones who had noted our arrival in the area. They dealt with our small squadron HQ with a surprisingly professional thoroughness. They used incendiary and armour-piercing bullets and came in low again, again and again, until they had left all three of our lorries ablaze and put one of our armoured cars out of action. Trooper Dunne was hit in a lung and died, but was, amazingly, the only casualty. During the attack, Wilson suddenly called up from the driver's seat to report that he'd left bonnet-cover open, could he get out and close it? I prefer not to relate my reply. We spent the rest of the day watching the sky for their return to finish us off while the lorries roared and crackled with exploding ammunition. Plumes of flame rode skywards with enough smoke to give our position away for miles around.

The weather had suddenly become unpleasantly hot. We even felt quite sorry for the German working parties we could see digging away in the shimmering distance. As for the local going, it took Rod and me seven hours to cover sixty-six miles on our round of the 'A' Squadron troops on Easter Day. But it was a comparatively pleasant occupation after sitting amongst rocks waiting for the fighters to come back. They never did. I imagine they thought there was no reason to do so; but at the time we were not to know. I started reading *Mansfield Park*, so soothing compared with reality. The enemy were becoming increasingly aggressive. The Royals had begun withdrawing before German tanks, fifty of which were reported moving to our right rear (shades of Louvain). The Foreign Legion fired on the Royals, who replied with interest, and indignant messages could be overheard on the R/T. Peter Willes picked up the crew of a crashed Wellington bomber which they had set on fire. Charles Morrison-Bell returned safely from a trip to liaise with the French, and asked me if I would like a pint of Pimm's in a pewter tankard with a frog on the outside of it – three parts ice and plenty of cucumber and mint. 'I thought you might,' he said, 'though I haven't one to offer.' In the increasing heat one felt the flies crawling over one's face and exposed skin. Meanwhile the fifty tanks had swelled to eighty.

From then on it seemed to be a case of dogging the advancing enemy columns awaiting their pleasure, shadowing them and reporting every smallest detail. For those in reserve, however, there was some welcome cover that we hadn't come across before in the desert – clumps of scrub with some quite high bushes and one particular wadi, which reminded me of a good fox-covert, in which armoured cars could be hidden without resort to camouflage. Two 109s flew up and down it one morning for two whole anxious minutes, but gave up and flew away. No more enemy planes troubled us for the rest of the day.

On 7 April our particular Germans halted and on the 9th suddenly turned east and started off 'with oafish disregard for the luncheon hour' at exactly 1 p.m. Charles Gregson and Rowly Beech got as far as Tengeder, now well behind the enemy's advanced units. They thus found out their numbers and type so that when they turned slightly north we were able to hand them over with a full description to the Royals, who had been tagging another large column about Mteifel. All the time the enemy were relentlessly moving in, feeling for our main line of defence. They must have begun to wonder just how much longer they were to continue meeting only a handful of stand-offish armoured cars. These were the final stages of the build-up to the Battle of Gazala, where the winner of the build-up looked like being the victor in battle.

Meanwhile the Luftwaffe were forever overhead. The first German spotting plane would come over soon after 8 a.m. and the first spotting fly would land on one's nose ten minutes later. The planes continued to keep an eye on us unchallenged, but the flies were swatted in hundreds. As a troop leader rather wearily remarked: 'You would think our pilots would take off if only to keep cool? But perhaps they haven't got anything to take off *in*'. In spite of the heat, Wilson worked away unflaggingly on the none-too-healthy engine of our new armoured car, even with snatches of song. 'Can it be the moon?' he would suddenly ask at the top of his voice – pause for some tricky mechanical problem – then: 'Oh, no it isn't the moon. It's love in June!'

On the 10th the enemy column at Temrad actually withdrew after being heavily engaged by the Gunners. But although the 110 was surprised by the amount of flak (all of which missed it) sent up by our Free French neighbours, it only meant that within the hour the Free French were being intensively bombed. In our job, unless you were fairly certain of hitting an aircraft, it was wiser to keep absolutely still and quiet and hope to be allowed to continue 'to see without being seen'.

The early morning was the best time of day. Sometimes, tearing across some salt-pan at 60 m.p.h. at 5.30 a.m., it was cool and glorious. With the rising sun wobbling on the blue-grey eastern horizon, the squadron looked rather like a flotilla of torpedo boats, fanned out and black against their white dust-tails. But having taken up our positions, the heat would soon take over, the 110 would come moaning along, the flies would crawl and zizz and the fighters, too, were active. William Browne-Clayton got a bullet through his R/T set from one of them, but no one was hurt.

On 16 April we were introduced to the *khamsin*. This felt like a strong wind that had burst out of a white-hot oven. It virtually laid you out. The tinned butter was like boiling beer when it was opened in the evening. What water we had was hot. We gasped for air, sweating as though we were in a Turkish bath. I heard Downton tell Wilson he thought it might snow.

Our Tobruk water was so salty that we tried boiling ration biscuits in it before making tea, but the tang remained. Rod and I went our round of the troops, getting smothered in our own flour-like dust, wafted over us much of the time by a following wind. We did it again next day (forty-five miles) and had some difficulty in locating some of the cars in the dancing heat-haze. Across the browner areas they looked like towers or steeples in a landscape only broken by non-existent pools and lakes. The *khamsin* would die down only to rise again unexpectedly to send loose camel scrub rolling across the desert with empty petrol-cans and bully beef tins. It also blew away vital things like maps and code-lists which had to be chased and caught. Then we would collapse under our cars where lay the only shade.

I had a bath that evening at about 8.30 p.m. when things were cooler. A bath? With two mugs of water one stood with each foot in a separate sawn-off petrol can. If one filled a sponge and squeezed it over the head, very lightly soaped the body, then picked up as much water as possible from the tins, it was possible to squeeze, with the help of the reserve mug, enough water to rinse. It does not sound much but it was wonderful. I remained naked and as wet as it was possible to stay until night fell. The temperature had been such that the evening stew had been cooking away on its own to become revoltingly uneatable.

Johnny Henderson was shelled from the Teilim Hills while trying to shoot up an enemy gun south of our old RHQ area. The French lent us two guns which were towed up to help and the result was a draw. Meanwhile Peter Willes got well into enemy territory and cut as many of their telephone wires as he could find. (HQs had lines laid across the surface of the desert as soon as they reached new positions to ease the traffic over the R/T.) And the evening news informed us that HMS *Hermes*, two more of our cruisers and 'all available aircraft' ('That might not be many,' someone observed) were lost off Ceylon to a large enemy naval force. 'We scored a near miss on a cruiser.' 'Well done,' murmured a tired troop leader, just in from several days' patrolling.

On the 19th Rod and I had just completed our round of the troops when he called me across to his armoured car and asked me to let him be the first to congratulate me. 'As from now, you are the adjutant.' He wasn't joking. I rather supposed, even hoped, it would not be at all long before my unsuitability for the post would see me back with 'A' Squadron. As things turned out the job was to last through the next eventful and often critical eighteen months, right through, in fact, to the victorious conclusion of the North Africa campaign. So off I had to go, desperately sorry to leave Rod, Wilson and Downton.

7
Adjutant

RHQ was cosily concealed amongst some high bushes well to the south. Having moved in, I as quickly moved out with my predecessor. We drove right the way back to the transport where, for our hand-over, we sat amongst files (and flies). 'Reports on Officers' soon caught my eye and I discovered that I was 'level-headed in an emergency' (not otherwise?) and 'probably a suitable squadron leader'. I was equally surprised to read that a brother officer, who would have died of laughing, was 'a probable regimental commander'. However, on going through this particular file later the same day, I found that I no longer featured! My personal report had been removed. My immediate reaction was to feel very homesick for honest 'A' Squadron. A voice within me said: 'Go carefully. You are temporarily fallen amongst the career boys.' But apart from this, by the end of the day I had an inkling of what I was in for, and even ploughed through 'Establishments' with the RSM at 'B' Echelon. I hated that sort of thing, but at least it made a change. So did the pleasant company of Bill Mabbott, QM superb. And I slept till sun-up, enjoyed a leisurely shave, and breakfasted without accompaniment of Luftwaffe engines, actually sitting on a chair at a table. Then I drove back to Forward HQ as adjutant of the 12th Lancers, arriving simultaneously with General Messervy, commander of 7th Armoured Division. He was to take over from 1st Armoured Division, the KDGs to relieve us. The General had Robin Hastings with him, whom I remembered from Stowe; and he stayed on after the General had gone. It was a relaxed evening – until German tanks came on into 'A' Squadron's sector, to within sight of Rod's HQ. Fortunately, they turned away to the west before dark.

Mick Lindsay and Toby Whetherly of the KDGs also called in. RHQ was very social and I soon learned that whenever anybody visits a regiment the first thing they do is to ask for the adjutant. Furthermore the take-over directly involved me in paper work and operation instructions, dealing with certain aspects of the Army that I knew very little about. But I was thrice-blessed in having a paragon of an orderly room sergeant. His name was Rex Ingram. A slim, fair, intelligent young man, he, thank the Lord, looked after me through all the months to come. He was never upset or put out, fed up, depressed, flustered, ill, frightened or lacking in humour. Like Sergeant Arrowsmith, he was another guide, philosopher and, above all, friend. Nor could I have been luckier in my successors to Wilson and Downton. Sergeant Nutting, who had taught us Morse at sea, was an A1 operator or he would not have been holding such a responsible position. Corporal Booth, my new driver, was not only intelligent, but his quiet, dry sense of humour, after a while, became almost essential to my contentment. But, of course, a lot of paper began to come my way. So I devised my own 'desert filing system'. I dealt immediately with the vital, and matters of possible importance in the near future went into the breast pocket of my shirt. Such things could not, therefore, be forgotten for even a day.

A tame flycatcher inhabited the high bushes in which our cars were now so satisfactorily hidden. He or she visited us regularly and had no fear of man, hopping delightfully from the colonel's hat to my knee and onto the intelligence officer's map. The latter, Gerald Churchill, did not look much like a soldier, but was a very good one, with an admirable sense of humour. Then Charles Gregson chose this innocently rural moment to arrive with a really dreadful little Italian officer which his troop had just overtaken and bagged. The colonel's reaction: 'Throw him back, he's too small,' was interrupted by a call from 'C' Squadron who had just waylaid two German lorries and a staff car.

'With what result?' asked the colonel.

'We have the lorries, but the staff car tried to drive away. We emptied three belts of ammunition into it. It has stopped, but no one has yet got out of it.'

'Well,' said the colonel, 'are you surprised? I want identificaton now.'

Alas, four 109s then came over the scene. They wounded the troop leader, Ferguson, and six of his men. But his prisoners were sent back in a lorry under escort.

The following morning introduced something new into our lives, an artillery duel. All squadrons were impressed by the efficiency and ready cooperation of 4th RHA. Later, I was to discover that their commander was the Jack Christopher who had, with really unbelievable generosity and trust allowed me to ride what was plainly a *good* horse of his, round a hunter trial course on Salisbury Plain, years ago.

On 28 April the RAF reported 200 enemy vehicles (MET) and 'tentage' at Bir Tengeder. It was Charles Gregson's troop that was sent to confirm or otherwise. He took his troop to the Tengeder well itself after a patrol of some fifty miles. He reported the place 'all clear' which, at the time, was vitally important. It is so easy to write about. But having to retrace his steps

– or wheelmarks – through fifty miles of enemy-held territory cannot have been a picnic. The troop leaders of 1942 always made it look as if it was.

After this another interruption came in the person of Dick Bromley (who had come to us from the Warwickshire Yeomanry) who had with him a German major, Rudolf by name, and his staff car with its driver. This was a valuable prisoner from Army HQ and this time the colonel did not jest. Major Rudolf was grateful when I handed him back the novel he had been reading and, after searching them, the big leather wallets full of his things. There was also a magazine of scantily-clad females. Although he was sitting down in the back of a truck, he crashed his heels together. Then, with a laugh, he handed me back the magazine. 'My driver's,' he explained.

On 1 May the 12th Lancers pulled out and covered 100 miles, arriving at Meliba next day. From there we drove north to rejoin 1st Armoured Division, and a tent was erected on the barren sand. I was faced with a pile of work, while others made the most of a richly earned rest. Soon after our arrival George Kidston (commanding the KDG) and Bill Carr (commanding 22 Armoured Brigade) swept up in 'a dashing white staff car', an American utility type with the superstructure sawn off. They came to see how we were getting on, as an important battle was in the offing and our 'C' Squadron was to be under Bill's command.

A propos of this I was called to Divisional HQ. While I was there a severe sandstorm hit the area, cutting visibility to less than ten yards. I could only hope it would abate, since I had to get back. Meanwhile Rex Hitchcock (9th Lancers) entertained me in the mess and offered bed and breakfast, which I had to decline although the storm in no way lessened. By dint of sitting on the bonnet so that the front wheels kept either side of the telephone line from Division to 12th Lancers, I reached my orderly room tent before darkness. Both my driver and I were caked in sand.

Next morning was dull and cold – the blessed influence of the sea. I was writing, when a muffled explosion rocked the leaguer. We were all too used to bangs, but, so far back, this sounded wrong. I found Trooper Smith of 'B' Squadron with a hand blown off and his chin in a dreadful mess and Trooper Golding with one hand badly hurt with the bones showing. They had been examining an enemy 2-pounder shell.

A messenger arrived and, amongst other things, brought a list of those 12th Lancers taken prisoner at Chor Es Sufan on 28 December, fifty-six names to confirm our own list. Also twenty armoured cars were to go to Cairo for repair and 'A' Squadron was chosen to take them. I drove over to tell them in Major Rudolf's car. On receipt of the news they became like schoolboys being told they were breaking up early and, in the thick mists of the following dawn, they roared away, leaving the regiment depleted to say the least, with the commanding officer and part of 'B' Squadron already in Cairo.

On 15 May 'C' Squadron, under Bruce, went to 22 Armoured Brigade and out of our jurisdiction. Thereafter RHQ moved alone to the sea at Marsa Luch. As adjutant, it was like having a saddle and bridle, but no horse. I love the sea, having been brought up beside it and in it and on it. I went for a swim when I felt like it. I walked along the beach in the evenings with the blue-green Mediterranean crashing and booming ashore in rollers of Chinese white. Great fans of spray fountained up from the rocks. It should have been perfect. Yet I wasn't happy, though things improved the morning Jack Hamilton-Russell put his head round the flap of my orderly room tent. He had become adjutant of the Royals, who had moved into adjacent dunes, half a mile to the east.

'Come and dine tonight,' he said. 'In your outboard!' I accepted gratefully – and but for keeping the roaring surf on my right as I walked home afterwards, might well have had very considerable difficulty in locating my bivvy.

Some inquisitive enemy aircraft had taken to strafing our camp shortly before dawn. On 26 May, after a night of considerable air activity, one plane found us and decided to stay. I got out of bed and looked out. It was a Junkers 88 and although it eventually straightened out and flew away over the sea, experience warned me that it would very shortly be back, much lower and with guns blazing.

Almost at once I heard its engines growing louder. As it approached the shore it opened up, but the pilot cannot have seen the Beau Geste-like fort about which our tents were scattered. He flew his aircraft straight into its tower. It almost looked intentional. The burning, exploding wreckage of his plane hurtled, bounced and rolled, at least half a mile without touching anything but sand.

Picking up the bits of its crew with a party of HQ staff for burial – there was no one else to do it – left me strangely unmoved. When all was finished, however, and I had sat down to breakfast, I suddenly got up again and hurried outside. I was all right. It was just that I was unable to face any food for forty-eight hours. We established that the plane flew from Greece. A nasty scorched, sweetish smell hung over the camp all day.

At 1 a.m. next morning a roar of machine gun fire once more 'brought me from my bed'. It was another Junkers 88 sending a stream of tracer bullets right through our camp. Fortunately there were no more casualties. But the message that reached us that morning: 'Instant readiness for action' hardly seemed necessary. The commanding officer had only just returned from

Cairo. We were sitting in the mess when his eye came to rest on Rupert de Zoete. 'Rupert,' he said, tongue in cheek, 'are *you* ready?'

'For anything, Colonel,' came the reply.

'Then prepare my boat for the sea!'

That same day the Italian Ariete Division attacked Bir Hacheim, but was repulsed, losing the best part of fifty tanks. The Germans, however, made a wide detour south of the place during the night and struck north at first light of 28 May. At 2 a.m. I was again roused from my bed by a Junkers 88 hosing tracer vertically downwards. In spite of the fact that once again nothing and no one was hit, it was becoming a very tiresome interruption to our night's rest.

The colonel went in to Army and returned with the news that General Messervy and his HQ 7th Armoured Division had been 'captured piecemeal' and that the German 90th Light Division was already just south of El Adem. (Unknown to us and within only sixteen hours, the General and his staff escaped.) Then William Browne-Clayton arrived also from Army the following day. He told us laconically, that 'no one was worried – yet' and that '50 Division is still west of Tobruk'. I liked neither the 'yet' nor the 'still'. He also added that the RAF had bombed and strafed the Free French and had returned reporting 'a good day'. There had been desperate fighting south west of El Adem and about Hacheim 'where the unfortunate French have been ordered to stay to the last man and the last round'.

The next day the enemy appeared to be short of petrol and a French column joining up with 4th Armoured Brigade to the north had destroyed twenty-five immobilised tanks. The 4th Armoured Brigade went on and wrought havoc on the enemy's lines of communications.

That sounded more like it, but on 30 May a gap of ten miles was opened in our line after 150 Brigade had been attacked on all sides for thirty-six hours. On 31 May I was ordered, unexpectedly and to my delight, to take a convoy of thirty vehicles to Cairo, and was pleasantly surprised to meet a continuous stream of useful-looking traffic moving up to Knightsbridge, including 4th Hussars. There was no sign of a flap and all reports were optimistic in spite of the unavoidable confusion in the battle area caused by the dense dust-clouds. We also met our own 'A' squadron returning after their refit.

On 4 June the RAF came into their own and it was said that they destroyed thirty aircraft, including 'most of the available Stukas'. But by 5 and 6 June the failure of our counter-attack and the German defensive victory presaged worse things. Bir Hacheim was again heavily attacked on 6, 7 and 8 June and the situation began to look black. During which time RHQ was working round the clock (within sight of the Pyramids at Mena Camp) to get the rest of the regiment back up to the desert. This was accomplished by 12 June the day after the final evacuation of Hacheim.

After this Tim was lucky to get a fortnights' leave to Beirut, then a place of peace, comfort and beauty. Staying with some friends in the Hotel St Georges, he seemed to have had a very happy and relaxed time, not bereft of delightful female company.

Back in Cairo we took the road for the desert that same night, travelling up with 'C' Squadron which had recently come back from Knightsbridge and had now completed its refit. During our absence Tobruk had been lost and the enemy had advanced nearly to Sidi Barrani. We leaguered for the night at Bagush and were accurately bombed, the Luftwaffe flares turning night into day. Next morning I headed into the desert, making straight for Herbert Lumsden's Divisional HQ and, while there, heard that the Colonel, Peter Burne and Gerald Churchill (intelligence officer, but acting-adjutant in my absence) had been taken prisoner. They had driven up to a convoy of British vehicles but had found themselves surrounded by Germans (A vast quantity of British transport had been captured in Tobruk.)

The colonel's capture left a somewhat embarrassing situation at Regimental HQ, until George Kidston arrived as commanding officer. Although he was too modest to say so, Tim really was in command during this very tricky time.

Returning from Divisional HQ, we left in a hurry and took the road back towards the enemy with the task of finding our own HQ before dark at a new map reference (they had had to move while we were away) in open desert. And however comparatively calm it might be there, 'chaos' was the word to describe conditions on the coast road. There was a full moon, the Luftwaffe was dropping flares and flying up and down the road bombing and machine/gunning, and trying to get back to the regiment against a flow of stem-to-stern retreating vehicles was far too reminiscent of the last days before Dunkirk. But by leaving the road earlier than we intended and following the desert railway for twelve miles and the North Star for a further two, we finally arrived by calling for a tracer bullet to be fired skywards. How thankful I was to see it near at hand!

Getting out fresh orders for 'B' Squadron to move at dawn (to cover the approach of infantry to a certain line) ensured that I got no sleep. Furthermore, the enemy appeared to be 'waltzing' through our very extensive Matruh mine-fields and sure enough the order to withdraw was not long in coming.

That morning an RAF Hurricane was shot down over our heads by a 109. It was murder. The 109 was like a hawk attacking an old turkey and we were helpless to do anything about it. But at last we got back to Kilo 31 on the road to Alexandria and, as a regiment, pulled off the road for a hot meal. This must have been the nearest thing to the end of the 12th Royal Lancers (if only a temporary end) in regimental history. I was handed a plate of stew and mug of tea and sat gratefully down, gazing at the sea and thinking nostalgically of the recent delights of Beirut, when half a dozen shells shrieked over our heads to crash into the sea beyond the road. Half a mile to our south, some British vehicles were moving east along the top of the escarpment and my immediate reaction was that they must be trigger-happy. But then, as the saying goes, all hell broke lose. They started machine-gunning and their shells began to bracket us.

I threw away my lovely stew, poured my tea into the sand and did quite a commendable swallow-dive into my turret. There were men running to mount everywhere. We got back onto the road and away down it, firing smoke-canisters as we went. The resulting screen would not have discredited a destroyer. That and our speed saved us from being cut off. Neil Speke was wearing a panama hat and it showed clearly ahead through the pall. Even amidst the turmoil, it made me laugh aloud.

When we reached Kilo 60, patrols of 'A' Squadron turned and formed a protecting screen through which the rest of us passed. Mine had been the leading car when we turned off for our hoped-for hot meal, so I was one of the last to go through and not sorry to do so either. John Clark-Kennedy for instance, was with Corps, still inside the perimeter and must now be cut off. For by dawn the enemy were well to the east of the evening's scrimmage, with 'A' Squadron reporting them as 'coming on'. Indeed they were, at such a pace that we were soon racing them, literally racing their screen of twenty armoured cars. They caught up with one of Dick Bromley's cars, but in the heat of the moment, the crew got away. So fast were they going that, although they were travelling across desert and rather north of east while we were going due east along the tarmac of the Corniche, on, as it were, the rails, they kept level, their shells bursting to our right front. The contest slowed when they got to Fuka's landing ground and began looking for fuel. Two squadrons of the Queen's Bays, with Honey tanks then temporarily joined us, and a few hours later they were able to give great assistance to the New Zealanders.

We were very near Daba, which had always been the first port of call on our way back from the desert, the first taste of anywhere remotely civilised. But the realisation that if you breakfasted there you could easily lunch in Alex, was now no longer an encouraging thought. The fact that the enemy had temporarily paused to fill up from the dumps at Fuka did not mean that they were going to delay overlong. Hurricane aircraft were rising like wasps from a nest, as they took off from Daba landing ground. They flew away east, increasing the now customary feeling of being left on a limb. But at least John Clark-Kennedy rejoined us, his car having been blown up and burned out on a mine while still inside the Matruh perimeter. He had got out in the moonlight through 'a hellish crossfire' and might have stumbled into the middle of a German leaguer in the thick morning mist 'had I not observed a fat German having his morning squat'. He had taken avoiding action and made it to our lines.

Rowly Beech shot up some lorried infantry in the evening. They came bowling down the main road without a care in the world, unlikely forerunners of those who had begun moving on from Fuka, until Rowly's concentrated fire gave them a truly shocking surprise. Another surprise to me was the intentional but nevertheless sudden blowing up of a whole ammunition train in a Daba siding. The whole night sky slowly glowed blood red and then followed one of those bangs which shift one's very vitals. Unperturbed in any way, a Brigadier Windsor climbed up onto my car and said he had a South African battery of 25-pounders. I told Rod, and he soon had them straddling the Alexandria road. The 12th Lancers acted as his OPs, ensuring that the Corniche was shelled in the right places at the right times at first light.

And so, in the damp and misty dawn of 30 June, we came to El Alamein, just another railway halt in the desert between Daba and Burg-el-Arab. During the night 'A' Squadron had been temporarily passed rather than overrun. All their troops were still reporting normally. But their Squadron HQ had been reduced to one car, and it joined us carrying Rod, Neil (now 2i/c), Sergeant Major Knight and an Italian colonel and two of his whippers-in, who had evidently been carelessly over-eager to enter Alexandria. Behind, driven by a 12th Lancer trooper, came their staff car, a smart conveyance, we thought, for such scruffy passengers. But as Mussolini himself was already reported to be getting 'a white charger' forward to ride in the triumphal entry into Egypt, they might have been forgiven for thinking they would be rescued in the next day or so.

Rod told Neil, his only available officer, to watch the road. In silence Neil walked to his car, took a kitchen chair off it (this unusual piece of furniture must have been picked up at Daba) carried it some distance along the road, set it in the middle of the tarmac and sat on it. Folding his arms and crossing his legs he peered intently down the miles of empty road. That he thought the precaution unnecessary was obvious. But Neil Speke, enthroned in splendid isolation upon a kitchen chair in the middle of the tarmac, was my first and abiding memory of what was so soon to become a very famous place.

8

The Alamein Line

A composite squadron was immediately formed under Rod's command. Those without vehicles were sent back to Cairo. 'B' Squadron had brought the enemy column on to the above-mentioned South African guns. When German shells started to crash into the Alamein Box, we were ordered to move into the desert.

Through burning vehicles and exploding dumps, we bumped along to join 1st Armoured Division with bursting radiators and with many vehicles having to be towed (in a following wind). This was a particularly disagreeable trip as the hot and dust-filled air became suddenly thick with buzzing insects of cockchafer size which kept smacking into our goggles and against our faces. But once down in the desert we no longer felt alone and I put on pyjamas to go to bed that night. It was a delight to hear the enemy's attack along the railway had 'come to nothing' and that 'their tanks had been engaged' *by somebody else*. I suppose it is the same whatever formation you are in. But too often it seems in battle that only your own lot are doing something about it. To hear, or better to see, tanks going through or guns coming up was a rare uplift for the spirit.

On 2 July at 4.30 a.m. we moved back north to Gebel Bein Gabir. We were once more in sight of the sea. One squadron of tanks (9th Lancers) went past towards the enemy and a squadron of our bombers was also seen to be flying in 'the right direction'. There were other fighting units here, there and everywhere. A hatless officer in shirt sleeves was standing up in a staff car leaning his elbows on the top of the windscreen to watch us pass. I recognised from his photographs the Army Commander, who had taken over control, General Auchinleck. I thought he looked reassuringly unperturbed. I also wondered what it would be like to be bearing the entire responsibility for the defence of the Nile Delta. History has already shown how his handling of the situation not only stopped the rot but how, there and then, the tide began to turn. Imagination boggles as to what might have happened had the enemy been able to complete the extra fifty miles and reach the Suez Canal.

In the morning, the crashing of a Messerschmitt 109 at our very feet made a nice change. Dick Bromley got a 'left and right' at two Italian biplanes, even sending a third smoking out to sea. There was much enemy shelling of El Alamein station, but the New Zealanders collected 305 German prisoners and 35 guns. The RAF was now much in evidence.

Neil reported that a Messerschmitt 110 had shot up a lorry wounding one man 'but it departed in flames itself'. This was the eleventh lorry 'A' Squadron had lost by air attack and I could see it still burning as night fell – when, even as late at 7.30 p.m., twenty-four Boston bombers flew over towards the enemy.

Next morning the RAF shot down four Stukas directly above us, immediately after which a Kittihawk, with its nose painted to resemble a shark's, crash-landed in our midst. The pilot was all right and, having been restored with strong cordials, was sent to the rear.

The 9th Lancers squadron that we had seen the previous day now reduced three enemy tanks to flames and at one time the 4th Armoured Brigade had 200 enemy infantry advancing towards them with their hands up. No longer were we out in the open desert with limitless miles in which to manoeuvre. The Army now had its right flank on the sea, its left on the Quattara Depression. In brief and unofficial jargon we were now 'blocking a gateway rather than swanning'.

Once again we came under 7th Armoured Division. Artillery duels seeming continuous, booming and banging even into the night. My own chances of sleep were further impaired by there being a telephone line from my armoured car to Divisional HQ. If having to get out of bed after a busy day to speak to the Divisional Commander personally at twenty minutes to two in the morning was not exactly fun, it showed that at least things were afoot and that somebody was 'doing something about it'. Indeed, somebody was, for on 6 July Tat Brinton himself took 'B' Squadron on a special mission towards Fuka, now well behind the enemy lines. John Richardson, telling afterwards of their return from this raid, said, 'We went so fast we nearly took off!'

It was on the following day that George Kidston arrived to take command and the enemy started to advance south-east in order to straighten their line. This necessitated another withdrawal so, with the South Africans on our left and the New Zealanders on our right from the Quattara Box, we moved east for five miles. I was therefore speaking all day to our three squadrons and the transport on the R/T and Division on the telephone, and everyone who came near us asked to see the adjutant.

Thirty German tanks, MK III and IV, came roaring towards our right, black diesel smoke puffing from their exhausts. My own reaction was to run and keep running, but better men in tanks and behind guns stopped them. Towards evening, four German vehicles containing 'what must be extremely

brave men' (Robin Brockbank's description when reporting their move-
ments) tried to come on alone, but were easily stopped. Further north 89
Germans and 'no less than 300 brace of Wops' were captured. Although the
latter figure when applied to Italians was to become commonplace, it
sounded a lot just then.

At 10 p.m. I had to send back a long encoded message over the air. This was
a not unfamiliar task. The operators were, of course, more than capable of
doing it, but it was the officers who did the passing of important messages
because, if anything went wrong, it was their responsibility.

A voice would come up over the R/T: 'Hullo MEME, BOBO calling. I have
a message for you. Over.' The listening operator would reply: 'O.K. Over.'
Back would come the order: 'Put an officer on the set. Over.' 'O.K. Off.'

But the sending of long messages at night or at last light could be a
marathon. First, the atmospherics were usually appalling at that hour. Sunset
could be the worst of all. It meant having to shout at the top of one's voice
coded stuff such as: 'Monument nuts playbox Pedlar' etc. through a wild
mixture of what sounded like an Egyptian funeral, dance music and the
foreign tongues of announcers. A very faint voice would answer 'Say again all
after "monument"'; and thus might it go on for well over an hour. It was
extraordinarily exhausting, but such messages were literally matters of life or
death. Men's lives depended on their accuracy.

I had been asleep for ten minutes when an alert sentry shook me, in more
ways than one, with the news: 'Tanks advancing, sir. Enemy flares less than a
mile off.' But my ears had become so practised I could recognise the squeak of
a Cruiser's tracks or the rattle of Bren gun carriers. Similarly, I had learnt to
tell the difference between German flares and ours, the former so much bigger
and better. Also the knocking of a machine-gun turned away from one was
quite different from the double 'smack-bumb-smack-ack-ack-bumb bumb'
of those pointing at you, i.e. the 'smacks' of the bullets through the air and the
'bumbs' of the distant shots. I went back to sleep.

Nevertheless as dawn broke on 11 July, we had to move a further eight
miles eastwards although 800 enemy were taken prisoner and we heard that
the Australians were doing great things in the northern coastal sector. The
General again rang me personally on the telephone. Was I 'sure that there was
no enemy east of the 87 easting grid?' Having already reported that area
clear of enemy, it went against the grain to have to check with the troop
leaders. I knew from experience the extra annoyance one could feel when,
having risked life and limb to get accurate information, and having obtained
it and sent it back, one's word was doubted by people in comparatively safe
areas. 'A' Squadron asked me to tell 'the Great Man' that although the grid

line was not actually marked in the sand, he could rest assured the enemy
were still '*exactly where we said they were*'. But a commander has to be
certain and such irritations, though rare, sometimes had to be suffered. I also
think that our reports being discounted for too long at Chor es Sufan,
resulting in the capture of fifty-six of our own men, had made us a bit more
touchy than some others.

Neil took over 'B' Squadron the next day and at the same time the front
perceptibly quietened down for the first time since we had reached Alamein.
But only for twenty-four hours. The foe became once more aggressive and
troop leaders were now pinpointing 88s and 105s. In the north the enemy
penetrated the Alamein Box, but were seen off by South Africans. They tried
again next morning and the South African armoured cars on our left began to
withdraw. I had the forward link mike in my left hand, the telephone to
Division in my right hand and was dictating to Sergeant Hartley on the rear
link. I felt rather like some sort of tycoon until eighteen Stukas came over us,
keeling over into perpendicular dives straight at us. They hit a lorry, but there
were no casualties, nor did the lorry burn.

On 15 July 3,000 prisoners were taken; Neil's squadron shot up lorried
infantry, with Dick Bromley conspicuous as usual; and though our troops
were shelled 'by 88s, 105s, 75s and 25-pounders', we moved forward during
the next two days. A newly arrived subaltern reported: 'They are shelling us.'
Pause. 'And we are shelling them.' The commanding officer thought this
deserved congratulation.

Now the fly plague began in real earnest. Even in a strong wind they settled
on us in clouds – indeed a wind seemed only to make them more comatose
and clinging. One wiped rather than flicked them off. When life became
extra-busy on 19 July they were of quite considerable nuisance value. George
Kidston now had under command the 12th Lancers, one squadron of 8th
Hussars, one company of the Rifle Brigade, a battery of Royal Horse Artillery
(Essex Yeomanry), two troops of RHA anti-tank guns, a detachment of
Royal Engineers and a field ambulance. The plan was that we should sally
forth and get at the enemy's landing grounds. Bill Carr was the brigadier in
charge. So, in the afternoon, we left the Wadi Regil and moved east to join his
4th Light Armoured Brigade.

Suddenly there were far too many vehicle states, personnel returns, lists of
minimum requirements, etc., etc. for my liking. Bill Mabbott was away sick,
which doubled, even quadrupled, my task and I missed him painfully.
However, by 6 p.m. things seemed to have been sufficiently tied up to allow a
visit to 'B' to find Neil. All was ready for the off, with morale in 'B' Squadron
very high. I stayed for dinner, a four-course affair with as much drink as one

might have found in Shepheard's bar. Considering time and place it was a hilarious party: Neil, Tat Brinton, John Richardson, Matt Abraham, Dick Bromley, Charles Gregson, and Rowly Beech were very good company. When Sergeant Nutting drove me fast across the cool, moonlit desert to my own armoured car a mile or two away, I quite felt as if I had been on leave.

At dawn we moved forward to wait for a gap in the line. This recalled a picture which hung in the mess before the war, depicting men and horses in a snowy France, called *Waiting for the Gap*. As we sat up on our turrets with the R/T endlessly crackling away, grating out messages, and with the flies in their thousands swarming all over everything, I longed to get on.

Various requests began to arrive from some of the attached, but none from 8th Hussars under Shan Hackett, self-containedly content to 'look after their own'. Our column started off northwards in the evening and a long ride through the moonlight ensued. The codeword for 'I am stuck' was 'Kilkenny,' for 'halt' 'Cork'. By the time we reached our destination I thought I never wanted to hear either place mentioned again. The word for 'I am moving' was 'Waterford' and, better still, 'I have arrived' was 'Wexford'. When everybody had said 'Wexford', we got two hours' sleep.

This sortie was to coincide with an attack in the north. Waiting for the latter to materialise, we sat and roasted in intense heat. The flies formed a thick black scum over the surface of one's tea and blackened any food; one could not keep them from one's face, bully beef and tea simultaneously. Dead or dying, they had to be scraped off everything in sight. We endured like this until 29 July when we moved sedately back to our start point. The attack in the north had failed and 1,000 Australians were said to be missing, although a German infantry regiment was reported as having been 'wiped out' by 69 Brigade.

George now decreed that I must take over all 'Q and admin' of our group. From then on, therefore, I had two forward link cars, a rear link of my own and a telephone. If a troop leader wanted something, it now appeared that his request must pass through seven different HQs. This was rubbish, so I cut it down to size.

Rod's eyes had been troubling him and, now that our sortie had come to nought, he was sent back 'to more civilised climes' as Shan Hackett put it. Shan himself suffering from sand-fly fever, went with him, and even Neil was quite a sick man.

My diary describes 30 July as a 'day in Hell', which referred to the heat, flies (now pestering us with the night), administration work and to the fact that I was now temporarily technical adjutant and signals officer as well. At dawn I drove to Brigade for details of another 'boldly conceived plan' to go through the Quattara Depression past Siwa, presently held by Italians, and up between Sollum and Matruh, some 1,000 miles in all. If it came off we could do much damage, but at the time I confess I thought it fairly improbable that many of us would get back. Meanwhile we remained in observation of the minefields about Himeimat, a flat-topped hill standing on its own at the southern end of the Alamein Line, on which the Germans frequently had an O.P. for their artillery.

There was a change of wireless frequencies on the night of 6 August. Everyone was to be immediately notified of these changes but not over the air in case of enemy interception. As the signals officer was away at Division and the technical adjutant was stuck in soft sand six miles away, the responsibility fell on myself and Sergeants Nutting, Hartley and Ingram to go 'bowling round in the pitch black', as Sgt Nutting put it, looking for the various squadron signals sergeants. We set off to the accompaniment of heavy machine-gun fire to the north and the occasional flash across the sky followed a couple of seconds later by a rumbling bump. Just as we had finished and there was a suggestion of dawn, the signals officer arrived saying he had got stuck in soft sand 'three times for one hour each time'. I sent him to park his jeep and get some sleep. He drove away and I heard a crash as he went over the escarpment. It was evidently not *his* night either.

'C' Squadron had come out of the line and Bruce asked me to dine. Neil picked me up and we drove across together. It turned out to be Mark Wyndham's twenty-first birthday. There were also present Robin Brockbank, John Stimpson and Geoffrey Nares. Nothing matched the pleasure of those little desert parties. For here we were, stuck far out in the Western Desert a matter of a few miles from Rommel's leading troops, without so much as a tent. But we were kindred spirits who had been together for some time, resulting in that desert camaraderie which was so helped along by shared danger and hardship. We each felt certain of the others' complete reliability.

On 12 August we had, of all things, a rehearsal for a withdrawal. We had to pack up and waste (in our view) a whole morning sitting up on our turrets waiting for the order to pull out. From 7 a.m. to 1.30 p.m. we sat there, the driver was at his wheel, the operator at his set. We then covered twenty fly-blown miles across scorched dust, in which the cars either stuck under one in the deeper sand or nearly drove one's spine out through the top of one's skull over the sand-hidden rocks. Having reached two hideous conical hillocks (known officially and unattractively as the 'Black Paps') I answered a string of calls from people who were stuck with boiling engines seizing up or breaking altogether. When most of us had got there we were immediately ordered back to where we had started, but too late to make it before dark. After covering the last four miles under the stars, the familiar escarpment loomed out of the darkness. We went at it independently and as fast as we could. But only three cars got up. The rest had to go round trying for better going. An uproarious night followed of howling engines, wasted petrol, and, because of interference, top-of-the lungs conversations over the wireless with the still scattered squadrons. The same night the Indians put in an attack to the north-west of us and the consequent din of shellfire presently added to the crescendo. I was not alone in thinking what a good thing it was that it was not the opposition doing the attacking.

That rehearsal was the silliest thing I was ever asked to do during my military career and my diary of August starts: 'Everything thrown out of joint by yesterday's farce. "B" Squadron was not "all on" until 10 this morning, much of our stuff being still stuck 20 miles east of here.' But by nightfall (and a miracle) Colonel George and I were relaxing with a copy of the *Hampshire Chronicle*, lent to us by Regimental Sergeant Major Harper, who lived at Winchester. George was in good form and voice, reading aloud the accounts of weddings and whist drives in a broad Hampshire accent. Upham, Hursley, Wherwell, King's Somborne, Hurstbourne Priors – I read the names of the familiar villages, all with nostalgic memories.

Then 'B' and 'C' Squadrons relieved the 11th Hussars, leaving 'A' Squadron and RHQ to suffer what is now universally and all too often referred to as 'bull'. The new divisional commander was coming to visit us. This charming one-armed Rifleman who had recently been promoted major-general, drove round in a jeep and shook hands with everyone. The soldiers looked very smart and clean as they stood strictly to attention in spite of eyes and mouths nearly black with flies. The latter no doubt added to the chances of getting Gyppy tummy and indeed Bruce and I were struck with it. My diary notes: 'Whereupon there was a flap and everybody moved back eleven miles!'

Some sunrises were quite incredibly beautiful. The desert very slowly turned yellow with pale green and blue shadows in the shallower hollows. But it would have started deep blue and its later transformation from violet to pink, never quite the same, was worth waiting for. Then it was a white glare with the flies mustering their unbearable forces. My head was opening and shutting. I had nothing to take to relieve it. Sergeant Ingram said he needed 'a blanket and surcingle ride' but such a thing might have killed me out of hand. News came that Geoffrey Nares was on the dangerously ill list in Cairo – only twelve days after Mark's birthday party at which he had been such a zestful member. It was not so much a blanket and surcingle we needed as less tinned food, heat and flies and more fresh fruit and vegetables.

Robin Brockbank's troop successfully shot up an enemy observation post, while I was forced by a large and painful swelling beside my right eye to wade through deep and dirty sand to the MO's staff car. I had a temperature of 104. The MO, Patton, was perfect. No stupid questions, but straight into the back of his car to privacy and peace for the rest of that day. He had my bed-roll carried across and I slept away from the sound of wireless sets. Next morning he gave me a local anaesthetic before cutting my swelling with an ordinary blue Gillette razor-blade. There was a bit of a mess, but I felt so much better that I returned to my job – to hear that Geoffrey had died. Neil was now evacuated sick to the main dressing station and I started having such pains that I had to go back to our MO. But after two days' rest I felt better and returned to work inside a mosquito net. It was stifling, but it kept off the flies.

And so that fairly awful August petered out. I felt a new man. So did Johnny Henderson, or so he said, when he returned from leave in Alex. Charles Morrison-Bell returned from the Delta with a new sponge for me and three bottles of John Jamieson, not entirely for me. High overhead, two tiny silver minnows streaked across the sky, ME 109s on reconnaissance and clearly up to something. I began to get that familiar feeling of impending trouble. Sure enough I was woken that night by an unhealthy amount of talking (at such an hour) on the forward link. Gerald Churchill had been replaced by Michael de Piro as intelligence officer and assistant adjutant, and he had become the best of assets. So, as I already completely trusted him and had been ill and was whacked, I just lay where I was, only half-listening. But by degrees I became fully awake as I heard footsteps approach my bed through the sand. The enemy was starting to advance through the minefields near Himeimat. This was in 'B' Squadron's sector.

I got up and saw the great wobbling German flares hanging over the minefields and at 1 a.m. took over the forward link. We were supposed to be able to hold the enemy for four hours. Thanks to Neil (who got the MC for his trouble), and his 'B' Squadron, they were held for sixteen hours. Twenty-two enemy tanks were burning, nineteen damaged and at least a dozen had gone up on mines. Then the weather went mad. A *khamsin* raised a dust storm that reduced visibility to five yards and through it we moved to Mseilikh (no more than a map reference), 'B' Squadron somehow shadowing and delaying the enemy all the time. By evening, however, the enemy was just east of our old dwelling-place, the Wadi Ragil. Here was yet another of those nights when the desert seemed filled with the roar of engines. That Rommel was making a very determined bid to drive straight to the Delta appeared only too obvious. But were those his engines passing endlessly all through the hours of darkness? Not on 'B' Squadron's front but what about elsewhere? Hard to tell in the distance. Like the night at Haseiat after Chor es Sufan, I wondered just what daylight would reveal. In fact daylight only brought four ME 109s which, fortunately for us, were evidently just 'having a look'. Then we joined Brigade at Gamus, from where we watched the RAF at its best. Every forty-five minutes their bombers arrived overhead as regular as clockwork. Out of 150 enemy vehicles on our immediate front only 30 were reckoned unscathed by their bombs. The 8th Hussars destroyed a further 50 and 'killed between 50 and 60 of the enemy during the morning'. As we returned up our escarpment, our bombers continued to pulverise the enemy into the night.

The latter now turned north, presumably to attack the New Zealanders on the flank. As we now know, they were expected to do this. Rowly took prisoner an NCO and five men of Trento Division under heavy fire. By the evening of 3 September a westward movement became discernible amongst the enemy. Next day Dick Bromley took prisoner a foxy-looking German officer and two of his thugs while the RAF 'slipped up' unwittingly by attacking my old troop and wounding Sergeant Arrowsmith. (Slipped up – in those circumstances it must have been nigh on impossible to tell friend from foe.) On 5 September our patrols got back westwards through the minefields, once again to be held up east of Himeimat. It was back to square one. The whole affair became famous as the Battle of Alam Halfa. The enemy had had a good try, but got thoroughly punished.

We had heard that a General Montgomery had taken over the 8th Army, but we were naturally sceptical. Generals had come and gone a-plenty. This battle, however, bucked everybody up and his 'No withdrawal, no surrender' message had impressed even us.

When George and I paid a visit to Neil's forward patrols on 6 September, approximately thirty shells crashed into the area of Dicky Hezlet's cars while we were dismounted there. I remember rolling myself over and over and grovelling at the bottom of a small slope. It was the cars they were shelling, but that did not make any difference to us. (The only difference it made to the cars was that Dicky had splinters in his blankets the first night he tried to sleep in his bed.) As soon as there was a lull, George and I beat it. In mitigation, we were only in a jeep; even so, I felt rather ashamed. John Richardson got blown up on a mine, which took a front wheel clean off his car, but no one was hurt.

While visiting Peter Willes's troop with George, I saw the nearest Germans send up purple smoke as Stukas flew towards them. Our own ground-to-air signals never seemed to be understood. I once frantically flashed the letter 'G' on my Aldis lamp at some Hurricanes. But they circled and circled us until I thought they would run out of fuel, before flying away. But the Stukas altered course and, seeing 7 Motor Brigade nice and near, came plunging down on them instead, setting several vehicles on fire. As we departed, Peter's troop began to be shelled by 105s. Our Gunners, however, plumped a shell slap onto the top of Himeimat and the shelling ceased. That shell must have discomforted if not destroyed the enemy OP for the top of that little hill was a small area. It was a marvellous shot. By 8 September the battle had become something of an anti-climax to those on the spot, though the history books have now told us why pursuit did not follow victory. Three ME 109s dropped one bomb each on our HQ vehicles for breakfast, but hit nothing. Then Bill Wainman called about the 11th Hussars taking over from us at the end of the week. Tony Crankshaw was now his adjutant. Having joined together fresh out of Sandhurst, we had become the adjutants of our sister armoured-car regiments and it made all the difference when it came to things like hand-overs. For all the accompanying mirth, I think they went more quickly and smoothly. Having handed over to the 11th, we heard with delight that we were to go to 10 Corps under Lieutenant-General Herbert Lumsden, a *corps d'élite* designed to give the *coup de grâce*, we were told.

Flies were just about smothering us so Ingram and I sat in separate nets in the orderly room truck like a couple of gladiators. Into these nets arrived a message from the GOC saying how the 12th Lancers' performance had been of 'the highest possible order'. We knew it had, but it was nice to have it confirmed. The 11th Hussars relieved us and we were also given a farewell by fifteen Stukas and their escorting 109s without any damage whatsoever. Immediately after which a Tomahawk came careering in along the ground, causing us much more anxiety than any Stukas. It was crash-landing through our vehicles in a spectacular slide, a bow-wave of sand and quite a few sparks from buried rocks. The pilot climbed out unharmed, a charming boy, bare-headed, in shirt-sleeves and drill slacks. He was indignant at the suggestion he might have been shot down. 'Lord no! Is there a scrap on?' He had 'engine trouble' . . . We gave him a large gin and tonic and sent him to the rear in one of our trucks. Corporal Booth, my driver, suggested that if we went on like that we would have 'formations of the beggars flying in on purpose'.

At 2.30 p.m. we left the Samaket Gaballa and I cannot say that I had been unhappy there. In good company you can be happy almost anywhere. But for sheer discomfort, it won hands down. And this was simply down to the flies.

We were far enough back to be safe, even from the Luftwaffe, when we eventually drew rein later that evening. As we halted, I turned to watch my old 'A' Squadron speeding up behind out of the west like the Young Lochinvar. As they swung into line without seeming to decrease speed, I remembered another picture in our Aldershot Mess. The 12th Royal Lancers apparently charged the Inspector-General of Cavalry (as the finale of his inspection), pulling up on the haunches in perfect alignment but rather uncomfortably close to the Great Man. The caption had read: 'Very dashing, Colonel . . . [I-forget-who]! But be pleased not to do it again, sir!' I could not resist picking up the mike. John Kennedy answered. 'Very dashing,' I said, etc., etc.

We reached the Delta's edge, at Khatatba, after 137 dusty miles, just as the sun was setting. It was Sunday, 13 September 1942, and a phase in our desert war was over.

9

Alamein

To be really busy is neither to know nor care what day or even hour it is. Signing a mere 200 passes in order to get the majority of the regiment away on leave without delay was a tiny sideline. Work in the orderly room tent would go on until nearly midnight and once or twice until 2.30 a.m. I had one end portioned off as my sleeping quarters. I did a lot of visiting (DAAG and AQ for example) and altogether achieved about one tenth as much work as Sergeant Ingram and Corporal Davy. Meanwhile others who had spent much of the past nine months at the sharp end were able to unwind a bit. After a while things began to settle down and Neil and I dined with the Royals one night and the 10th Hussars the next. But by 23 September, just one month before the Battle of El Alamein, the division began practising night marches through minefields and, concurrently, I began to suffer from eyeache (from a kind of fever rather than overwork). Mercifully it wore off of its own accord after three wretched days.

It did seem that one operation order would arrive only to be followed by another which could be almost entirely different, headed 'Amendments'. These would be accompanied by many maps 'until only my head was showing above the paper involved'. About 4 p.m. we would set off as a regiment into the desert to rehearse moving by night, enjoy a good little meal with friends while the moon rose, then away we would go on a twenty-eight-mile march (in armoured cars, of course) through the moonlit sands. We would finish and get to our beds by 1.30 a.m. and rise again at 6 a.m. in order to be back at camp before first light.

On one of many visits to Divisional HQ I was able to enjoy the spectacle of a big whirlwind blowing down their officers' mess on its way to demolishing a neighbouring tent which was chock-full of maps. The sight of upwards of a couple of hundred of these seriously inconveniencing the ever-circling 'white-hawks', high in the sky, was as entertaining as all the *Tatler*s, *Field*s and *Country Life*s which soared over from the wrecked mess like driven pheasants.

At the same time there was an aura of smartness. The regimental guards of 9th Lancers, 10th Hussars and Queen's Bays were immaculately turned out, while ruler-straight lines of whitewashed stones began to sprout from the desert sand. Coming away from the GOC's 'lecture to all officers' was like leaving Sandown Park after a Grand Military meeting for all the familiar faces, and more than once I went to sleep to the silvery notes of a hunting horn seeing off guests from a neighbouring dinner.

It was decreed (General Montgomery now commanded 8th Army) that officers should do physical training. Somebody was so misguided as to construct a vaulting horse. Its life was very short. At the conclusion of a guest night before it was ever used, there came the crash of splintering wood and a few shrill cries of 'who-oop!' which told of its demise. It was not replaced. But we always managed to be on parade for PT even without a horse, though some of us may have breakfasted on iced beer. I once passed Tat Brinton on my way back to the orderly room, washing outside his tent as nature made him. 'September morn!' was all he said.

After one exceptional evening with the 10th Hussars, I looked like being thirty seconds late for PT. But not only had George Kidston been dining with the Bays, there was also a thick fog. The fixture was abandoned.

It could be genuinely foggy early, presumably, because we were so near the Nile. But next morning turned out clear and, very soon, hot; at the same time the turnout of several young officers was not considered by Colonel George to be up to standard. Nor was it. So I was told to drill them during the heat of the afternoon. As I watched them, fresh out of battle and at least three of them with Military Crosses, marching zestfully up and down that dusty stretch of Egypt, I thought of their contemporaries doing nothing at home. My admiration for them caused me to halt and dismiss them after only ten minutes.

Then the new Army Commander paid us a visit, General Herbert Lumsden accompanying him as corps commander. Immediately after they had gone, I happened to be on the telephone to Security Intelligence GHQ when my orderly room blew down. I was trying to hold up one heavy tent pole while still shouting into the telephone 'Is that Security Intelligence?', while my commanding officer was trying to hold up the other, yelling: 'Turn out the guard!' Being nearby, the guard not only turned out but had the thing up again in two minutes. George told me it was a '*habood*' (he had served with the regiment in Egypt before the war) or, in English, a sudden fierce duststorm-cum-whirlwind.

On 4 October Colonel George told me to take four days' leave. I handed over to Michael de Piro and made straight for Alexandria and the sea rather than for Cairo. *Here Tim had four sybaritic days with Teddy and Nora Peel in their fabulous house, where they dispensed unbelievably generous hospitality to a seemingly endless procession of officers on leave.* When the time came for me to drive myself back to the 12th Lancers, my depression at having to do so was slightly alleviated by the sight of so many RAF planes in the sky.

Soon after I got back General Dick McCreery visited the regiment alone. George being away, it was my duty as adjutant to show him round. It was just a social visit to his old regiment and I almost forgot that he was Chief of Staff, until we had completed our rounds, when he suddenly stopped. I supposed it was about time for one of those conundrums that accompany such tours, and I knew I would be found wanting. 'How is your mother?' is the question he asked me. I have never forgotten that, nor him.

Jaundice had become a sort of officers' disease. No one could quite guess why officers got it while the rank and file appeared to be immune. Anyway, Colonel George now succumbed and Rod Palmer took over at this critical stage. As things turned out, he was to have the very considerable responsibility of commanding the 12th Lancers throughout the coming Battle of El Alamein. It helped me to understand what it must have been like for my father when, as a major and at equally short notice, he had had to lead the Lancashire landing onto the Gallipoli Peninsula.

As the battle approached, paperwork eased off. We had, however, to make another practice passage of the minefields by night. This night march was a dress rehearsal for Alamein, now less than a week away though we did not know that at the time. But it was as well that we got home before daylight for, with it, came a severe sandstorm mixed with driving rain. It was painful to the face and cut visibility to nil. But at least Khatatba had one virtue – a lack of flies.

Two days later we rose at 5.30 a.m. and moved out as a regiment through the darkness. As we had then to wait for Divisional HQ to move through us on the Cairo-Alex road, I had time to purchase a good breakfast at the Half-Way House and enjoy it in the company of Rod, Neil, Michael de Piro, Tat Brinton and Matt Abraham. I shall always remember that breakfast and the people with whom I shared it. In spite of the hour, the uncertainty and grey skies, everybody sensed great events just ahead and was in the highest possible spirits. No regiment could possibly have gone forward to battle in better heart.

The sky was positively speckled with *our* aircraft: twenty-five Hurricanes appeared to be doing formation drill overhead, just as had the German bombers at Carvin two years before. As no doubt it was intended, it was an encouraging sight. As we arrived in our new area, twenty-one RAF bombers roared over westwards escorted by thirty Kittihawks. But the best sight of all was that of seventeen Spitfires howling over, fast and high. There were flies to welcome us back, but it was late October and they were nothing like as bad as before. There was a pretty sunset, made prettier by eighteen Kittihawks flying out of it. The atmosphere that evening was of calm before storm; confident calm.

20 October dawned to the wholesome rumbling of a great many tanks, all British or, at least, British-manned. The whole Western Desert seemed to reverberate with British intent. Rod went back to Amiriya to attend a 'lecture by the Army Commander'. Meanwhile a large operation order arrived to be worked out with tracings to be copied onto our maps. Michael attended to the latter part of the job as if it were child's play, so that when Rod arrived back everything was prepared. All the officers were assembled to hear the plan of battle. It was thrilling listening. It was our first taste of the personal effect, many would say magic, of Montgomery. The 21st dawned with ME 109s so high in the blue sky they looked like midges except when one occasionally caught the rays of the rising sun to flash silver for brief seconds. Michael continued to deal with the map work, which was very considerable, allowing me to cope – just. At 1 p.m. the regiment moved to its assembly area just west of Ruweiset. I liked moving. The moment we were stationary, the telephone would be swiftly hooked up and the questions begin.

The great day arrived, 23 October 1942. Even in those impeccably sane and well-run surroundings I was given, at this eleventh hour, a completely new set of numbers for all the cars in the regiment. They were to be painted on 'forthwith' so that the military police, who were to shepherd us into the minefields, should know who everybody was. It was no good being angry. It had to be done. And perhaps it was not a bad thing for there was nothing more to do beyond waiting for the tapes to go up. It certainly kept people busy, but the language was robust.

That night it was practically full moon and very light. Everybody was in top form and Neil came over to say something rude in broad Geordie to which I replied in kind and in broad Hampshire. We then had a trial of strength and I remember slightly hurting my knee. It was an exciting evening. About 9 p.m. we pulled ourselves together and everybody got mounted. The ensuing artillery barrage, which soon began to blast the night to fragments, is history. To me it was one long, continuous rumble like side-drums being rolled and it formed a flickering, flashing accompaniment like the light playing on the ceiling of a firelit room. We travelled reasonably fast through the moonlight along Moon Route (the path through the minefields chosen for us) arriving at the front as 24 October dawned. Two searchlight beams forming a cross behind us were meant to tell us that the infantry had reached their objectives. As far as I could see they were crossed all the time we were moving up, but it helped morale.

A weary party of Gordon Highlanders was just coming back. Led by a tall officer, with kilted piper, they looked dirty and worn-out, but very fine. Perhaps it was the pipes but I had a sudden lump in my throat. But then it was no time for lumps in throat for we were being bracketed by 105s and 150 mm shells and the 2nd Armoured Brigade (our 9th Lancer, 10th Hussar and Bays friends) was held up by 88s and anti-tank guns. Less good for morale was the sight of the deep trenches with strips laid across them to lower in the corpses. The shelling, too, was deafening because we were now in front of the Gunners, between them and the guns of the enemy.

As we paused, a Boston bomber, one of an otherwise unscathed formation, must have had its steering mechanism damaged. I know nothing of aircraft, but, while its companions flew on, it began to dive, loop, soar up to loop again and at intervals of about eight seconds its occupants, one by one came rocketing out on the ends of parachutes. They were fortunate in that they would land inside their own lines. Michael and I watched in silence. It continued to pull out of some power dives, each one of which had to be its last, and the parachutes kept billowing out at the right moments. We prayed that the pilot's was the last, for what a hero he was. Out it came, the plane rolled over and, with screaming engines rising to a crescendo, went into one long dive, plummeting out of sight. A black mushroom of smoke rose up from somewhere near the Corniche – and the artillery banged on.

Another Boston, also flying in formation, was then hit. I do not much care for flying when every possible aid to safety is employed. But this was a bomber one second, a descending candle-flame the next, a torch which fell faster and faster. It accentuated the bravery of those bomber crews who were sitting targets for the German 88s. But at least the Stukas got a worthy reception by way of a change. At dusk they came weaving over and ran into a fountain of tracer from the 8th Army. Miraculously it failed to bring even one of them down, but I never saw fireworks to equal it and it was very good for morale. They disgorged their bombs 'any old how', their dives were shallow; and who could blame them?

25 October started with 12th Lancer casualties. Sergeant Major Robinson (he had been a lance-corporal in my troop at Penzance and rocketed to stardom in war) got shrapnel in his thigh and 'C' Squadron lost two cars on mines. Mainly owing to the churned up dust, visibility was poor, but the 10th Hussars drove off thirty-six enemy tanks to our right. At 5 p.m. there was an enemy attack 'in strength' against 24th Armoured Brigade on our left and the 10th Hussars came back south through us to help 'break up this attack

instead of launching their own proposed counter-attack' following their seeing-off of the thirty-six tanks.

A temporarily attached officer wandered over to our RHQ. We disliked being interruped.

'Any news?' he asked of Rod.

'Only that we're winning.'

Our visitor thought this over.

'How much by?' he asked.

'Two larks and a wren,' said Rod without looking round. The officer went away.

Now the 10th Hussars came through again, heading for yet another tank battle. The Stukas also came again, this time dropping their bombs 'without even dipping in salute'. But, by pure luck, they managed to hit an ammunition lorry which erupted into a spout of fire and rocketing stars, followed by a 200-foot sheet of yellow flame with scarlet edges which set two more lorries on fire. The three of them glowed red all night long, distracting us with loud crackling and intermittent explosions.

On 27 October there was another artillery barrage from 11 p.m. to midnight. In the morning we all saw, for the first time in two and a half years of fighting, a German ME 109 shot down by a British fighter, a Spitfire. All around us the entire area was smothered in British vehicles, not just those of the 12th Lancers any more. We had been wondering why we had to stay there, unless it be 'to add tone to what would otherwise have become a vulgar brawl'. Our troops were still out in front of tanks *after* they had joined battle, which seemed scarcely necessary as one of the affected troop leaders dryly put it.

Where RHQ was situated we were only getting 'overs', though those were not nice either. For example, an empty jeep was suddenly lifted up, turned over and put face down on the desert's surface as if by an invisible giant hand. Vehicles were constantly being consumed by shell bursts only to reappear, unscathed, when the smoke and dust cleared. Matt Abraham was in worse plight, pinned down behind 'a hummock, one foot high, two broad'. He had left his car and walked up to a ridge because any vehicle that appeared on it got blown up. He had already seen five tanks in flames on that same ridge. Now, having reached a position where he could observe the enemy, he was pinned down by machine-gun fire and it was half an hour before he managed to wriggle back to his car. But he was then able to direct fire onto the right place.

Another Stuka set an artillery limber on fire. It was a hundred yards from us and exploding ammunition was humming everywhere. As everybody seemed to be in the bottom of slit trenches, it devolved on the 12th Lancers to put it out – which they did just as Herbert Lumsden drove up in a jeep. My diary says he was 'very un-Corps Commanderish and in excellent heart'. Before leaving, he said that commanding a corps was 'easier than commanding a regiment with people like Tim, Neil and Bruce in it'. There was another deafening barrage that night prior to an attack by the Australians.

On 29 October we had to recce new routes for the 1st Armoured Division through minefields further north. Nineteen Stukas came slowly over at 10.15 a.m., just like the old days, and started a huge fire which acted for the rest of that day as a sort of magnet for bomb-dropping ME 109s. They came as moths to a flame and helped make our sector hell. Sand on the existing routes through the minefields had been ground into deep, fine dust which drifted like snow; to drive a jeep now called for four-wheel drive every-where.

On 30 October the battle seemed to have stabilised into artillery duels. They roared on and on and it was the first night ever that I got some sleep in a slit trench. First there was the night bombing which had disturbed recent nights and secondly our own barrages. Apart from being much safer, sleeping in a trench dulled the sound of the shells sizzling overhead, as well as the actual explosion from the cannon's mouth. In the morning, however, at 3 a.m. we set off with orders to 'keep going, not stopping for 88s or 105s or anything like that', which sounded slightly ridiculous, not to say suicidal. But as long as everybody else is coming along too, I thought, it might work. It was the right idea and anyway, I had a growing faith in the Army Commander. So after negotiating more minefields we arrived out into the open as dawn broke.

Of several vivid recollections concerning this debouching from the minefields, I can see now the silhouettes of the Priests – turretless Grant tanks with 25-pounders mounted on them – hurling shells after the re-treating foe, long tongues of flame licking forth from the gun-barrels and an all-pervading smell of cordite.

There is a slight break in the narrative owing to the loss of one page. But 5 November saw the regiment moving fast to Daba, where it was rejoined by Colonel George Kidston 'looking far from well'.

Charles Gregson charged an 88mm and a 50mm, captured both, took six prisoners and shot the rest who tried to shoot him after they had surrendered. How easy that is to write! But it was our view that men have been awarded the VC for less. These Germans were busy getting away at the

The author as trooper in the Life Guards, dismounted

The author as trooper in the Life Guards, mounted

Portrait of the author by his sister Molly

Morris CS9, 'C' Squadron, Villiers St Simon, 25 October 1939

Wash sketch by the author, 'Margate Station, June 1st '40'

The author with Colonel Kidston, 27 January 1943

The author on Beltra Boy, Kelso Show, 1967

The author, Limerick, 1971

expense of their allies, any amount of whom were left standing without transport.

We passed Daba station as the sun was setting. It was just over three months since we had passed through, going the wrong way on the night the ammunition train went sky high. Now, indeed, the boot was on the other foot, for this was the start of the 8th Army's advance which was to take it via Tripoli and Tunis to Sicily and up the length of Italy without a defeat. We did not stop at Daba, but kept going after dark, grinding along in single file. Our column halted now and again, and after one prolonged halt George dismounted and went to the head of the column. He found a truck driver (of another unit) asleep. This fellow had dozed off and allowed the vehicle in front of him to go without him into the night. George nearly went mad – and rightly so, for shortly after and directly because of this, as we crept forward through the darkness with a new lead car, we ran, literally head-on, into a German leaguer. The first thing I knew was when the bright green flares went up right under our noses, just like getting too close to the fireworks on 5 November – which very date this was! Simultaneously their Spandaus opened up, the tracer tearing white paths over our heads. Their aim was high (it is said that one shoots high in the dark) which gave us time to break up and make tracks before their mortars crashed onto where the column had been.

It was something of a miracle that we were all together at dawn. The latter part of the night had been eerie, with lightless vehicles creeping about the desert, none knowing friend from foe. Then came deluging rain to turn the desert into a quagmire and soak us to the marrow. We saw crowds, really vast columns, of resigned German prisoners being marched east, dragging through the yellow mud, often ankle-deep in water and holding groundsheets over their heads in feeble attempts to ward off the elements.

Bruce and Ned got too close to the Germans. It afterwards transpired that Rommel himself was in the column they attacked. But Bruce's own car was shot up, killing his Signals Sergeant Francis. The equally valuable Corporal Plant was also killed, leaving Bruce in the nightmare predicament of finding himself dismounted with Germans closing in. Ned Mann went to his rescue and managed to grasp his wrist but, because of wet mud, lost hold. Ned's own turret already had a 2-pounder hole through it, he had lost his operator and the enemy were surrounding him, so he had to keep going and he had to leave Bruce in order to do so. After which it was found that Sergeant Goodlow was also wounded and missing.

So it was good news that Dicky Hezlett had taken prisoner what he termed 'a bundle of Wops and their general' (he was second-in-command of Pavia Division) to whom George was 'courteous to a Black Prince degree'. He gave the general and his very Latin ADC our only tinned crab for lunch, using our 'utensils' and had water heated for them to shave. He called across to Rod: 'How about some lunch?' Without moving, Rod replied that he was only waiting for the opposition to finish with his plate.

'You'll be all right, sir,' I overheard his operator reassuring him, 'We have disinfectant in the car.'

I don't think it was intended as a joke.

By the following day the 22nd Armoured Brigade had reached The Wire and we heard that the Americans had landed in Algeria. They were coming to meet us! The news from home on the radio neglected to tell us that the British 1st Army was also involved.

Up to 10 November the 12th Lancers had taken something like a thousand prisoners and by 11 November plans were being discussed for 'a non-stop gallop' to Benghazi. The enemy was now reported out of Egypt and Rod and I had a swim in a glass-clear cove as we neared Sollum. My twenty-seventh birthday dawned most beautifully as we moved on at 5.30 a.m. The pale blue escarpment slowly turned to rose as we approached it, the dunes on our right already white against a navy sea. But from that fresh and dewy start we moved into a boiling landscape of dirt and dust, climbing laboriously up the steep escarpment and passing, half-way up, our own General Herbert deep in conversation with New Zealand's General Freyburg. We came to Fort Cappuzzo and halted on the road across that flat and featureless stony waste.

10

On to Tripoli

The new order issued here was that we were now to 'gallop to Martuba and seize the airfields'. This sounded 'just the job': we replenished cheerfully, gathered together and set off once again at 3.15 p.m. The enemy had blown the road and bridge, which we thought quite a compliment – it was usually we who did that sort of thing in order to stop them. Having somehow got across, a fairly horrible ride followed through a moonless night to El Adem. It was midnight by the time we got there, having passed one burnt enemy vehicle after another, wrecked aircraft, charred cars, graves and a number of recently and hastily abandoned Italian tanks, with their wireless sets switched on. Again we replenished in darkness suddenly riven by terrific flashes as an empty portée shot up some friends somewhere to the rear of us. In contrast to the day, it was very cold as we moved on, meeting a minefield at 6 a.m. but finding a way round it. We now had a battery of 2nd Royal Horse Artillery commanded by Len Livingstone-Learmonth (who drove himself in a jeep), with a troop of 6-pounders and some anti-aircraft guns as well as some Royal Engineers and Service Corps people. I believe we had some 240 lorries in all, but 'the pace was too good to enquire' all the way down to Bir Hacheim. By the grace of God we did have Bill Mabbott with us and they were his pigeon. How he controlled this unwieldy lot, keeping us moving and fed, remains a mystery. He was, as always, superb.

As we were coming up to Hacheim, the car in front of me was rocked by an explosion and ground to a halt in a fog of dark grey smoke. My immediate impression was that it was a shell fired from Hacheim, but it was of course a mine. Although no one was hurt, we swung away east and went wide round the south of the place. The French had not been exaggerating when they had reported destroying many tanks there during the previous May and early June. The whole area was littered with Italian M 13s. We did not stop to look, however, nor did we breakfast until 11 a.m. After which we covered a further 103 miles, reaching our old haunts about the Chorma Ridge north of the Teilim Hills where Rod had photographed the buzzard's nest and where the little wild flowers had bloomed in the wadi. I wondered if our tortoise was still there.

The sun was setting when I jumped down from the turret. It had been something of a marathon for the drivers, though I never heard a murmur of discontent. But we all got some sleep before moving at daybreak across the self-same terrain over which 'A' Squadron had escorted that raid behind the enemy lines the previous April. There was a thick fog, which we had experienced before in those parts, but when it became patchy, as the sun rose higher, a host of Spitfires arrived directly overhead and began to circle us. I flashed at them on the Aldis lamp the day's recognition signal (the letter 'G') for all I was worth and at last, to our intense relief, they straightened out and flew away.

We reached Martuba at 11 a.m. to find the enemy flown. But a formation was reported to have slipped along the Tmimi-Mechili track in the fog after we had crossed it near the Halegh el Eleba. I wondered if the Spitfires found it. Their pilots had done well, under the circumstances, to identify us, seeing that the advance elements of 8th Army were, in racing parlance, upsides with the Afrika Korps and all going in the same direction. There was no sort of battle line any more.

Now, however, the regiment scoured Martuba's five landing grounds and secured them so that the RAF could come safely in. The total bag of prisoners was 'five unhappy Wops'. And then it began to rain again in earnest. As I had bagged an empty German vehicle pit into which to tuck my car, I was soon parked in a sizeable pond. I moved to higher ground while the heavy rain continued all night and into the following day. Once again we were as wet as if we had fallen into the deep end of a swimming pool. Robin Brockbank and Matt Abraham reported the roads to Derna effectively blown and the latter had the misfortune at this stage to lose a car on a mine. But he came in at sunset with a further load, mixed this time, of Germans and Italians. Mark Roddick was now commanding 4th Light Armoured Brigade and only Neil's 'B' Squadron was to accompany it forward. This was mainly in order to provide wireless links over the especially long distances they were expecting to cover. But the rest of us were left sitting in the rain, taking stock. It was now at last that a kind of reaction set in to all the activities of the past months. One wanted to go on advancing without stopping, all the way home. Instead we had to suffer the dreadful anti-climax of not only stopping but remaining where we were round these landing grounds while the RAF flew in and took possession. The sad babbling of their Kittihawks' engines was an incessant accompaniment in a minor key. And they certainly took along the kitchen stove when they moved. Tents, caravans – Martuba began to look like Epsom Downs on a wet Derby Day.

On 20 November 1942 we moved south east back down into the desert, into open leaguer and on the flattest, draughtiest, stoniest bit of it. Yet I was to grow almost fond of the site. On the way there Robin lost a car on a mine and the following day the Army Commander announced his intention of lunching with us at 12.30 p.m. But he arrived some time after 2 p.m. having lunched in his car en route. By now, common sense overrode etiquette (it had so often had to) and we only waited a very short time before falling on the extra good viands. Montgomery was in excellent form – not really surprisingly – and it was encouraging to see him and discuss everything, even though our morale was astronomic too. It soon became obvious how admirable was this practice of his of getting to know his army personally.

On Sunday we were told we must have a church parade. The first hymn, so said the itinerant padre, was to be sung 'leaving out the fifth verse', which naturally focused all eyes on the omission. 'Time like an ever-rolling stream,' we silently read, 'bears all its sons away.' The text of his sermon which followed was: 'Our pillow is hard.' We knew that too. The following Sunday it was raining just enough to justify cancelling a second performance.

'B' Squadron's return to the fold only remains in my memory because I noticed the squadron leader's back was plastered in mud. 'Too much Chianti?' I suggested. Not so. He had 'got onto a pony outside Barce which completely got away with me and it seemed wisest to abandon ship'. But since I mentioned Chianti, he did happen to have brought back 300 gallons of it, and he invited me along to the 'wine-tasting.'

On 27 November General Herbert Lumsden called in. He was his usual immaculate, inspiring and cheerful self. But though we did not know it (nor did he tell us) he had really come to say goodbye. I did see him once again – in the Berkeley of all places – before he went to the Far East as a liaison officer for Winston Churchill. But this marvellous soldier, proven in European and Desert warfare, was killed by a kamikaze pilot during the Battle of Luzon while on the bridge of the British flagship. It was a cruel waste of a rare and remarkable man who could laugh with the young while holding high command. We, particularly, had reason to be thankful that he came back to command 12th Lancers (when the Germans invaded the Low Countries in 1940), having already handed over to another and returned home for promotion.

Jaundice had been taking its toll amongst the officers. Six had had it, now two more succumbed. Better news was that the Russians had cut off 120,000 Germans before Stalingrad and the Japs were in trouble between Buna and Gona. Our own advance had already reached Agheila. We ourselves had to be content with playing the 9th Lancers at football, having constructed a good flat field by clearing the scrub. Meanwhile Leslie Monroe-Hinds, who had joined us at Khataba (having returned from ranching in Argentina) was sent to Cairo, ostensibly for a course on 'The German Army' with a view to his becoming the next intelligence officer. But he took a 3-ton lorry with him to bring back the 12th Lancers' Christmas dinner and no one could have done a better job. It seemed unlikely we would be moving on before the New Year so it was a real chance to do things in style. We collected enough material from abandoned enemy landing grounds to build dining and rest rooms for an RHQ and an officer' mess about the size of a spacious loose box. These huts were the envy and admiration of all who saw them. We were becoming positively civilised.

But the new Corps Commander, Herbert's successor, General Sir Brian Horrocks, who now came to visit us, thought otherwise. He did not see the huts, which formed a sort of village for the whole regiment over the hill. Nor, unlike the Army Commander and General Herbert, did he stay for lunch. He had all the officers lined up before he left – and told us how absolutely frightful we were. We were 'taking no trouble whatsoever to give our men a good Christmas'; in fact it was quite clear to him that we did not consider our men at all. Had this been in any small detail true, General Herbert would have told us so, but he had been in the desert as long as we had and knew what was going on. Coming from an 'unknown' (to us), not long out of England, his address was considered in questionable taste to say the very least. Luckily our morale was unassailable after recent events – including Leslie's mission. If, sartorially, a certain individuality and lack of conformity had crept in, everyone was spotlessly clean and smart and the matter of dress in 8th Army was universally understood. General Montgomery himself was to write ' . . . I was not particular about dress so long as the soldiers fought well and we won our battles.' We didn't bother to enlighten General Horrocks about the essentials that he had missed.

Happily we were ready to go forward again long before the rest of the Corps and on 7 January 1943 we came – how gladly – under the seasoned and enlightened command of 30 Corps. The general commanding 1st Armoured Division came to wish us goodbye. He thanked us for all the regiment had meant to him, said how sorry he was to lose us and finished with these words: 'I disagree categorically with everything the Corps Commander said to you the other day and have told him so.'

After which our ride forward of some 600 miles to join 7th Armoured Division was a conscious pleasure. I sat on the turret top and revelled in all the greenery, the trees and bushes of Djebel Akhdar. The grassy plains reminded me of the wilder parts of Northumberland, especially when it became cloudy and tried to rain. I half expected to see someone hacking on to a meet of hounds or a training gallop marked out with sprigs of gorse. We parked for the first night on a garden-like hillside amidst stunted pines and the odd cypress. Soon after dismounting, I heard gun shots and presently Neil came along carrying a brace of chikor (hill partridge).

On again next day through country reminiscent of Dartmoor before dropping down a steep escarpment onto a plateau dotted with farms like little white boxes, in fields where cattle grazed and which were bordered by orchards. Then down even more of a drop to the coastal strip. This last escarpment had a picturesque old fort at its top, which gave the impression of riding through a picture from some old book of fairy tales. Having covered 125 miles, we stopped for the night near Driana and, with the sun still high, I went for a solitary swim at Solluch. I swam in the sea whenever I got a chance; for me there was no relaxation to equal it. On my return, glowing, Booth and Nutting had a delicious hot supper waiting, embellished with fresh vegetables. Later, Dick Bromley shot a duck. It was as good as being on leave.

Next day it was back into the desert for us as we moved to the south of Benghazi and took the road to Agedabia. Since it was raining hard, this had in places become a bleak morass into which vehicles sank to the axles if they strayed off the hard. The regiment religiously observed the 100-yard interval between their own cars, but this march discipline was eagerly taken advantage of by the vehicles of other units, who cut in and filled our gaps, nose to tail, all the way along the road. This made us all an attractive target for hostile aircraft, the very thing we ourselves were out to avoid. We covered 105 miles, reaching another Beau-Geste-like fort, Agedabia, at last light. In view of the fact that we had travelled 230 miles in two days along a road, no wonder that General Herbert had described our 150-mile ride from El Adem to Eleba via Hacheim in twenty-four hours across sand (and much of it in darkness) as 'a good forced march'.

In cold rain we continued on round the Agheila corner through the abandoned enemy defences and, after a further 125 miles, stayed the night among the bleakest sand dunes imaginable, a truly loathsome place. All the way there, other road-users had continued to fill the gaps between our cars. We wondered if these other drivers ever considered why the 12th Lancers maintained hundred-yard intervals. Evidently not, for one of these, while cutting in unforgivably, not only crashed into Trooper Hetherington of 'A' Squadron, but killed him.

We continued for 100 miles and found ourselves once more amongst wild flowers. I parked for the night in a fold of the ground that was a thick mass of tiny mauve and yellow blooms. Neil came along and had supper with me. Sitting amongst the flowers we had soup, lobster, the afore-mentioned partridges (one each), fruit salad and a cheese savoury. We shared a bottle of 'The Widow' and topped off the repast with Martell 4 Star. I thought that, for supper beside the road on the line of march, we had not done too badly. But as Neil once said, why be uncomfortable unless you absolutely have to be?

It was here that Colonel George Kidston once again caught us up, this time much better and looking more his old self. We came under command of 22nd Armoured Brigade and on 12 January 1943, after passing through Sirte, turned south into the desert. Here, on the 13th, as we were preparing to advance on Tripoli, the Army Commander once more came to see us, going informally to each squadron, so as not to interrupt final preparations after our long march. Before leaving, he placed on the sand beside my car some copies of a magazine – I think it was called *Soldier* – pointing out that he had autographed all the covers showing a picture of himself. As the squadron representatives called in I told them, before they left to take a few copies 'if they liked'. This pile of magazines remained untouched, the pages of the top copy ruffling open and shut in the breeze as we drove away for Gohsia. Today I really regret not having at least one copy as a memento, though I suppose they would only have got lost if under those circumstances we had taken them. But it was rather interesting that not a single copy was so much as opened by anyone at all.

'C' Squadron now did a few casts in the area where they were to take over. But they could not find the troops they were to relieve. Fortunately they were experienced, and therefore wary enough, to do this without getting a bloody nose. That they eventually relieved these troops without casualties was an admirable feat, considering the latter were not where they said they were. So all was ready for the advance and first light provided a spectacle never to be forgotten, in its way comparable with HMS *Repulse*'s farewell to the convoy in the Indian Ocean. White in the brilliant sun of a glorious morning, the tanks of 22nd Armoured Brigade came rolling up from behind us, spread all across the flat desert as far as the eye could see. They deserved massed bands, but the growing growling roar was really better. It was surely a sight and sound that would make the most fanatical Nazi get up and go. I had not then reached an age when one expects to be disappointed. So, even though the 8th Army had twice been driven back after getting only as far as west of Agheila, this time I felt certain it was going to Tripoli. For one thing, the Army Commander had said it was, and so far his forecast had been accurate.

Not really surprisingly the enemy in the north cleared out during the day, but at dawn he was still holding on to a landing ground where the coast road, the only road, turned north to Misurata. Two ME 109s made abortive hit-and-run raids on us, but this was a very different matter from the old days when groups of them would sail in as they liked, select their victims at their leisure, then stay up to forty minutes giving them the works.

Our task was to find a way over the Wadi Zem-Zem for the division. This was a rough, steep-sided old place and, luckily for our leading cars, not held by the enemy. But the going was shocking and mines were plentiful, so it was a pointer to the speed and therefore daring of these troop leaders that those of us coming along nice and safe behind were able to keep going at the same pace all day. No delays, and although the enemy were holding Dufan landing ground with 88s, 'C' Squadron was next day advancing on Misurata while 'B' Squadron had taken Dufan. Mark Wyndham, who was wounded in the neck and an arm by an 'S' mine, was evacuated. Denis Robinson was more fortunate. His car went up on a mine while he was riding on a mudguard (as from time to time we had all been inclined to do) but he was not hurt. I remembered the numberless times I had relaxed in the spare wheel, fixed to the front of a Humber. At the close of a hard day, when it had been a case of pulling back only a mile or so to leaguer for the night, Wilson would drive fast across some smooth, flat salt pan and it had been a wonderful sensation – nothing in front of you, the breeze whipping back, free from dust. And if there was no breeze, the speed made its own. But it was a pleasure I was prepared to forgo after hearing of Denis's mishap.

Now it was 'A' Squadron's turn to find a way over the Wadi Soffegin. Approaching it, we encountered an oblong rectangle of cultivation, green and lush. Being hunting men, I suppose, we went round it – thoughtful for the farmer. But many of the tanks did not. A pathetic sight was the old Arab who came limping from his tents, gesticulating wildly and to no avail. I wondered what the poor wretch would do for compensation miles from anywhere – and how he would feed his camels.

On 18 January we reached palm groves, lovely in the early morning, a sort of misty powder blue where they grew in depth. There were more cultivated plots guarded by man-made sandbanks strengthened by palm fronds stuck in along their tops. We were nearing civilisation. The Army Commander joined us here and leaguered with us. He wanted immediate and first-hand information and so my car was driven up beside his. I found him quiet and easy to get on with, obviously keen to capture Tripoli, but relaxed and happy that we and everyone else knew what we were about. Even the friendly rivalry between 11th Hussars and ourselves as to who would be first into Tripoli amused him. John Poston (11th Hussars) was one of his ADCs, our own Johnny Henderson being the other. Our liaison was one of unforgettable accord.

Dick Bromley took his troop forward with the 51st Highland Division to Homs. 'B' Squadron was at Cussabat and Van Burton charged twenty enemy lorries, shot up three and placed himself between the remainder and the rest of their column. Matt Abraham and Sergeant Gwilliam destroyed nine lorries, a staff car and a lorry with an anti-tank gun mounted on it, which came to try and tow the wrecked staff car away. But, alas, Sergeant Parker, one of the best, was killed in this action. After dark three bombs fell inside the tiny area of RHQ without damage. Being with General Montgomery, we were temporarily Army troops. That we were all un-scathed was almost unbelievable.

Although to reach Castel Verde across country had in the past been described as 'impossible,' Matt said he could do it. Indeed, 'A' Squadron moving all night, got there soon after first light on 21 January to find Matt already there. Just another of that officer's superb performances. As we in RHQ came to the place, a fat moustachioed Italian farmer in a homburg hat held up outstretched arms to try and stop us, but at this stage of the proceedings it was unlikely that any member of 8th Army would stop for anything Italian. Looking back to ensure no car was delayed, I saw why he had waved so desperately – he was being murdered right there on the road by Arabs. Perhaps he had under-paid them, been a hard master in palmier days, a misguided landlord? The cars came on without a glance and by evening we were twenty miles east of Tripoli; and there Peter Miller-Mundy rejoined us from England.

The enemy had blown the road again and again, always of course be-tween impassable dunes or where there was a cliff on one side and a sheer drop into the sea on the other. Apart from mines, these demolitions were also covered by 88s and machine-guns. The sappers performed mighty deeds that night and next day. As our tanks went rumbling through I noticed that Highlanders were draped across their engine-covers behind their turrets, a modern version of Highlanders holding on to the cavalry's stirrup leathers. But this was where we, on the coast, were forced tempor-arily to take a back seat while 11th Hussars, inland, led the 7th Armoured Division across open country from the south, entering Tripoli on 23 January. On 24 January we took over from the 11th Hussars and, by-passing Tripoli, carried on the advance westwards. We now came under 8th Armoured Brigade commanded by Roscoe Harvey, a 10th Hussar and a top amateur steeplechase jockey.

For just one afternoon, however, we had been able to lie flat out on *grass* after having *a bath*. I had heard cocks crowing, seen trees other than palms, gardens with flowers and even a hedge – which we agreed badly needed cutting and laying. We relaxed in the sun with eyes closed in green, calm, rural surroundings. For just one afternoon . . .

11
Mareth and the Left Hook

Taking over from the 11th Hussars, I saw Tony Crankshaw again. He was looking for a site where his regiment could leaguer after being relieved. There was no more open desert to choose from. Bill Wainman, now commanding, briefed me. 'It's a bit dangerous up there,' he said, jerking his head towards the enemy. The one road led straight into a palm grove and it looked suicidal to try and go along it in an armoured car or anything else. 'You don't see an 88 till you're on top of it,' he said, 'and, of course, you don't see it then either.'

The outlook seemed bleak. These groves would have to be pasted by the Gunners. All along the road were bordering palms, then a clearing, then more palms – no apparent 'way of traverse' as Henry de la Falaise would have put it. To begin with we were held up by demolitions covered by enemy 75s firing from Melliat. Ned (Mann) told me it took him 'seven times going forward and back, forward and back', before he could get his armoured car turned round after coming unexpectedly onto a crater and under sudden shellfire on that narrow road. But the Sapper sergeant with him, in spite of being wounded in the face by a bullet shattering his windscreen, got on with the job of getting the crater filled in.

At Sabratha, as it began to get dark, I ran down in the hope of an evening swim to the Roman ruins beside a dark green boisterous sea. In the shelter of the groves I had not realised that the sea shore was very windy. The ruins were desolate and mournfully eerie, as though there were ancient and unfriendly ghosts amongst the dark pillars. I hurried back across ground that had been anything but improved in that a good many of the Italian population of Tripoli, as well as their retreating army and the Germans, had evidently used it as a staging area, omitting to make sanitary arrangements of any kind. I am still surprised when I read of its charms in the travel advertisements. To me it was an evil place. We were forced to sleep in the area that night and we all caught fleas.

Then we came under command of 131 Brigade. This was an infantry brigade of high renown of which we were to see more later. The country was very enclosed and was certainly no place for armour. The infantry were marching up, dividing the road in single file, as I went forward with orders for

'C' Squadron. More rain flooded the craters, but Alan Carson managed to get around to the south across a country which reminded me of the Hartford Bridge flats or Beaulieu Heath. He reached Mellita. Then the enemy shelling commenced from six miles east of Suara, which was the next village along that awful road. This was merely part of the enemy's delaying action, which, with the terrain on their side, could be successfully effected with the minimum amount of troops. One 88 could stop an army. Dick Bromley's troop ran into an anti-tank gun and both he and Willett, his driver, were hit. Also I knew John Mountain, a cousin of Dick's and a new arrival, would be with him under instruction on this patrol. Dick died during the night. He had been first class, in the forefront for a long time and always cheerful and full of dash. This was on the approach to Zuara from the south.

Owing to demolitions to the east of the place we had had to use a railway track and I was stopped by two infantry carriers which had stuck, blocking the way. Ron Holman was also trying to get past with 5th RHA (ex-K Battery). Sunburned, filled out and with a moustache, he looked very different from the clean-shaven, thin and rather pale young man I remembered riding at most of the pre-war steeplechase meetings, partnering many winners. I think he commanded the Horse Gunners who performed the joint musical drive with the 12th Lancers at the last pre-war Aldershot Tattoo. But now we took two hours to clear the track and it was not until next morning that we entered Zuara. As we drove into the place, four ME 109s came down out of the sun dropping bombs rather than machine-gunning. They seemed to drop them haphazardly, clearing out immediately and doing no damage. We then cut the telephone wires from there to the west. While we were so engaged, the shelling by 105s restarted, suddenly, heavily and accurately. We dropped down the telegraph poles like trapeze artists at the conclusion of their act, straight into the shallow ditches on either side of the road, flat on our faces. They were deep enough. Though cars were hit by splinters, they were none of them put out of action and nobody received so much as a scratch. When the barrage lifted, we remained in the eastern outskirts, finishing our job on the wires and providing OPs for 5 RHA until we were able to reach the shelter of palm groves a mile further west. There would be no forward movement before dawn, so I raced down to the sea. No ruins here. No ex-Italian camps. No fleas. It was more like the desert of the picture postcards, white dunes, date-palms and blue sea. I swam. It was cold. I felt like a young lion afterwards.

We stayed there in close liaison with 5th RHA of which Peter Gregson commanded a battery. I remembered him riding Flying Lass at Sandown. His officers were a charming lot of horsy men. After another swim the second evening there, he asked me over to his HQ for a drink. As the sun went down and the flat Mediterranean turned silver-white, the subject of discussion was, of course, of all things, the trimming of horses' tails. One of their number had stayed in Hyde Park Barracks for some State function or other.

'I got one of their corporals of horse (that's a sergeant in those parts!)' he explained, 'to show my sergeant how they pulled theirs and what length they chopped 'em off! They're good at that sort of thing.'

Next day John Stimpson and Robin Brockbank were south of Pisida, only five miles from the Tunisian border. After an extra busy day Michael de Piro and I managed a quick swim in the semi-darkness while from Tripoli, now far to our rear, a scarlet curtain of flak rose slowly skywards in the shape of a fan. From where we were swimming, it looked impenetrable and, incidentally, rather beautiful. Then, on 4 February, Robin crossed into Tunisia in spite of enemy artillery still to the east of Pisida. But Van Burton (with Sergeant Gwilliam) and John Richardson both went silent over the air and nothing was heard of them after 12 noon. By evening RHQ had reached Regdalia, another bit of desert that recalled P. C. Wren's novels. Still there was nothing from Van, in spite of another troop shooting up a couple of Volkswagens in his area. John was back on the air, but by next morning Van was officially missing with his three jeeps (Bogskar, Billy Barton and Battleship). These were found burned out, though Sergeant Ritson's greatcoat and a letter to Van from a small sister were intact.

Four 88s were now holding Pillbox 44 on the frontier, but Robin and John Richardson were gradually working round them to the south. Meanwhile we heard that Winston Churchill was in Tripoli, which was nice to know, though operation orders for the next phase had now to be got out to squadrons. This was made more difficult by our move to El Assa being carried out in such icy, driving rain that it was not only nearly impossible to write down map references on wet talc, steering a chinagraph pencil with numbed fingers, but the going was so bumpy that the R/T kept cutting out. Vital messages were coming through in unintelligible spasms. Colonel George, beside me in the turret, was naturally eager to get back information at once, so that his 'Who is this you are talking to? Where is he? What's he saying? What's the trouble?' were questions unanswerable under those conditions. But we had to press on and only when we had pulled up in El Assa's one and only sandy street could I get everything clearer. It was comparative heaven – and the rain stopped, too.

There were horses at El Assa. Most of the population seemed to own a horse for they were tethered here and there along the street, saddled and bridled, with the big leather chairlike saddles I remembered the Spahis using at Olympia. And there were dogs. One poor dog loved us. He was a dear.

Grinning and thrashing his tail, he would have liked to join the regiment. But if any Arab came within twenty yards of him he became a dangerous wolf. He saw off all those who tried to approach my armoured car. But we only paused there to get the maps marked up and the up-to-date situation reports back to brigade. Then we moved on out of El Assa with the dog cantering beside us, tongue out. We were going too fast. I looked back and saw him stop. He stood watching us go as one's own dogs might when they know one is going away. His waving tail gradually waved less till it ceased its motion. It may have given me a slight lump in my throat, but one could not take along an Alsatian-sized dog in the turret of an armoured car.

At the start of 8 February we had a very unpleasant Stuka attack. None could be termed pleasant, but some were much nastier than others. Also we had been clear of them in recent days. Then Peter Willes's troop ran onto a 55mm gun, which scored three direct hits on his car. He was seen to jump out and try to crawl. Sergeant Sparkes was all right and managed to get hold of a tank to give support, but by then there was no sign of Peter, his troop or even his damaged car.

The Tunisian border, where we had to cross it, was more or less a boggy morass. With the help of the Sappers we all got over in single file and spent the rest of the day sending patrols towards Ben Gardame. In our new position my car was 100 yards from the brigadier's, so that he got a lot of information verbally, and therefore twice as quick. It kept raining and odd 109s were tiresome. Two of them came tearing over at 'mast-height' forcing me to kneel while en route to the brigadier's tank, but Sergeant Nutting emptied a drum from his Bren into them. The Queen's Regiment found a message from Van scrawled on a cellar wall in Pisida: '*All* well and well treated.' But apart from bits of his car and his hat being picked up, Peter's fate was still unknown.

Colonel George came in from visiting the squadrons wet and tired. He had recently added a 3-ton lorry to RHQ as an office, which was a wise plan. But he also used it as a bedroom and on this particular night it was late coming up. The boggy frontier, lowness of priority in the queue, shelling by 105s, and hit-and-run tactics by 109s, meant long delays for such vehicles. George was displeased to find he would have to sleep in a bivvy. Shortly after he had retired I heard muffled shouts and a strangled yell of 'God damn it, I've an apple-pie bed!' Of course he had not, but his bivvy was bulging and swaying and as Neil had just called in for orders for the morning and to sleep the night, he and I responded to the latest shouts of 'Help! I'm cast!' We each took a foot and hauled, drawing our commanding officer like a fox or badger. He shook himself and we all three adjourned to the back of the lorry, which had just arrived. I may have been wrong, but I could not imagine this happening to anyone commanding, say, a Guards battalion, and it all added to the levity which I think usually prevailed to some degree in our neighbourhood. Without a certain light-heartedness, such a life as we were leading – undiluted soldiering for literally months on end – might have palled a bit.

Friday, 12 February was a pig of a day. A young hurricane reduced visibility to fifty yards and put a generous layer of sand over every single thing. When Peter Gregson and Gren Smith-Dorrien (who was another I remembered riding a horse called Rathkeale in point-to-points) found their way to us saying 'We've called about the war'. I told them we could not get on owing to weather, mines, Tellers and 105s still east of Ben Gardane – 'So come and have a drink.' But Saturday dawned clear and, out of the blinding early sun, came a string of ME 109s to drop their bombs before scooting for home at hedge height (had there been any hedge). This made shooting at them dangerous for fear of warming up one's own good neighbours. Others, including presumably the latter, were not so unselfish. Bullets, which were certainly not the enemy's, came whining and ricocheting amongst our cars and chugging into surrounding bushes. However, one of the planes was set on fire and 'B' Squadron collected the pilot, a Luftwaffe sergeant, who said he had taken off from Medenine. After which their ground troops showed signs of leaving us and all night we could hear their vehicles groaning off towards the west.

Dicky Hezlett nevertheless had a car knocked out by a 50 mm as he entered Ben Gardane two days later. But although the enemy continued to shell the ridge in front of us, Ben Gardane was found to be clear very soon after Dicky's clash. Four ME 109s came swooping in at us and dropped their bombs on nothing before one of them received a direct hit and exploded in the sky. We reached the Wadi Fessi on sponge-like going where the ground sprang up behind us after sinking under our weight. Here I spent a dreadful night of shouting orders through a maelstrom of interference. It was almost impossible even to hear the acknowledgements. Had they received the orders or not? One had to be certain. It took hours.

Next morning showed the stuff of which our armoured cars were made. How they survived such terrain really was a bit of a miracle. We rolled, bumped, pitched, swayed and, indeed, crashed across high knobbly dunes with rocky protuberances all the way to the Nefatia road. Sergeant Scott reached Bou Ghara and destroyed a Volkswagen, killing two Germans and taking prisoner the wounded survivor. He then met sixty Italian irregular cavalry – 'Horsed,' he said, 'but only just.' They had no forage for the horses, no food for the men and no water. Scott alone disarmed all sixty, taking their rifles, revolvers and ammunition, and then told them to ride east. 'Don't leave the road. Someone will fix you up when I report your position.' Despicable as they were, we felt more than sorry for their horses as the sandstorm blew up again. We also felt sorry for our commanding officer who had to go all the way back over the knobbly dunes and the sponge in gathering dusk (and come back again afterwards) only to be asked, when at last he got there, if he would be needing any artillery support next day. For security's sake, they had not wanted to put the question over the R/T . . .

But at least the first sensations of spring were in the air as we moved up nearer to Medenine on 19 February. 'B' Squadron even got into the place, but was driven out later by the ubiquitous and deadly 88s. On the 20th George and I went to 'a sort of meet at point 104 between Medenine and the sea'. Other representatives had been sent from 7 Armoured Division, 22 Armoured Brigade, 131 Brigade, and RHA – so many familiar faces as well as friends, not seen since leaving home. 'We moved off [diary] to draw Medenine blank, but, as with an outlier, picked up a line and had a good hunt across the plough north of the place.' I remember German shells beginning to burst like a slow-motion film, grey flowers blooming, slap bang in the middle of our convoy. But all our vehicles, soft included, maintained the same pace, no panic-stricken zig-zagging anywhere. Sometimes the enemy guns appeared on the ridge to our rear (with a view to letting us have it over open sights?) but I never saw anything hit. It was, I suppose, a reconnaissance in force at which the Germans themselves had been so good before Gazala.

The next day we had 'Another fast hunt over much the same line, but this time over some big banks'. When we pulled up I remarked to George that it had reminded me of trying to get Diana de la Rue's old brown horse (which she was once generous enough to lend me) along with the Crawley and Horsham – slow and jumping well, but always behind! 7th Armoured Division was on our left, commanded by General Erskine. As he happened to be Diana's brother-in-law, George told him what I had said. Such infinitesimal things did, I believe, add to the family feeling amongst the armour of the 8th Army. As when, going up a long slope that morning, the CRA, Brigadier Friz Fowler, always recognisable with his Marmon-Harrington armoured car and his camel-hair coat, went through the motions of using a whip in a tight finish as he passed us. (He was to ride successfully in steeplechase again after the war when well past the age for such dashing activities.) It all made for cheerfulness and general camaraderie. I do not think that my spectacles have become rose-coloured. I wrote in my diary each day and my views are those of the time. And I thought then and know now that the 8th Army had a unique *esprit de corps*. People liked each other; I never noticed any jealousy and one was often very thankful for the help of others.

We could now hear the Italians on our wireless sets for the first time since Alamein. In contrast to the matter-of-fact short messages of the Germans, they sounded as if they had just been pulled out of bed and were going to burst into tears about it. I took half an hour off from the wireless and went for a walk. There were little Cotswold-like walls here and there and I brought back to the car a bunch or two of delicious young carrots which I found during my ramble. There was just a pleasant hint of civilisation and, passing through Medenine, this was strengthened by its Hôtel de France, Dubonnet advertisements and familiar posters. Here we go again, I thought, 1943 and *still* driving through French villages warring with Germans.

On 22 February we went forward to Metameur in lashing rain. When at last it cleared, we were surprised to see quite a high hill just in front of us, much higher-*looking* anyway than I had guessed from the map. ('Who put it there then?' I heard Booth ask Nutting.) While 22 Armoured Brigade, 51 Highland Division and 131 Brigade were moving up to the immediate rear of our patrol line, George spent an hour pointing out the lie of the land to the Army Commander. We went on up the road towards the Mareth Line next day, passing the high hill about which Booth had inquired. We were dismounted, talking to Robin and Matt in a shallow cutting, when a shell from an 88 burst on the road behind us. When we speedily got going, another hit the exact spot we had just left with an ear-splitting crack. We turned and tore back, literally chased along the road by shells from the 88 (or 88s?). I was never more relieved to get round a corner out of sight of anyone. With an 88, there never seemed to be a whistle or sound of a report. The burst itself was the first intimation and one of the many tasks of a troop leader was to report the exact position of an enemy gun or guns. Fully to appreciate exactly what that entailed, it was necessary to come under fire personally from one, or several, of them. Even as we pulled up in the hill's shelter, two 109s bombed us, streaking for home without staying to strafe, a new and welcome practice to which we were growing accustomed. We were glad to see one of them go up like a towering partridge before going into a spiral dive as a parachute billowed out. The pilot was brought to us and then sent back to the rear. One of the anti-tank guns must have muffed its elevation, for it lobbed our RHQ a shell for good measure. It was too warm a corner, however, for good health. So when the Army Commander told George that we were to go back to Ben Gardane to rest and refit ('but I want you back in the line by 20 March'), our spirits soared.

Before leaving, George and I went forward to Potter Miller-Mundy's troop – my own old troop with Sergeant Arrowsmith. 'A' Squadron was to be left under command of the Royal Dragoons, to rejoin us later back at Ben

Gardene. Two 88s gave away their position by engaging two Kittihawks and I could see two German tanks waiting at the foot of the nearest hill. To have tried to cross, in daylight, the intervening plain, without a scrap of cover, would have been suicide. With apologies to Kipling: 'The length and breadth of that grisly plain was sown with *Rommel*'s men, rock to the left and rock to the right, and low lean thorn between.' It was a perfectly marvellous morning, brilliantly sunny, but pleasantly cool without a cloud in the sky. Every wadi, fold and spur of the Matmata Hills stood out clear as crystal, etched sharp. The 2nd Gurkhas were in the area. They had gone into the hills during the night. There had been no sound but, according to Potter, they had come out at dawn 'smiling sweetly as they wiped the German blood from their Kukris'. We later met the 4th County of London Yeomanry on our way back, old friends of George who had come out to the Middle East with them. One got that fleeting impression of happy, healthy faces, which I had particularly noticed when the 7th Hussars trotted past Harewood on pre-war manoeuvres, the calm faces of the well-led. I also saw Wilson during our visit to 'A' Squadron, who told me his brother, a Sapper, had been killed.

Then we met 201 Guards Brigade moving up as we went back to refit. View halloas were once more exchanged, and one automatically found oneself thinking of Pirbright and Birdcage Walk. The Guards looked somehow so admirably typical of themselves – spotlessly clean, cap-peaks practically hiding their eyes, sitting bolt upright as to attention in their vehicles, formidable to a degree. 'With that lot between me and Jerry', I heard Booth tell Nutting, 'I reckon I can sleep sound in pyjamas tonight.' No formation could have been paid a greater compliment, even by Winston Churchill himself.

We arrived in our new area, a dead flat piece of land bordering the sea, without further incident. There were a few skimpy olive trees and some stunted palms scattered across a waste that was mostly sand but which had once known a plough. Neil's 'B' Squadron was on ahead, so he was waiting beside the road and waved down my car. 'I've found some white wine,' he said. 'It's Jewish and *poison*. Come and dine with the squadron and try some. I already have.' He pushed his hat to the back of his head closed his eyes and clapped a hand to his brow. There, and then, to our intense surprise, we were closely bracketed by shellfire. After which a furiously-driven jeep came tearing through the smoke. It contained a very polite subaltern of the Staffordshire Yeomanry, who asked us if we knew that we were 'on a range'. Equally politely we informed him that the Army Commander had directed us to this spot and invited him to move his range. It was rather dangerous, but perfectly amicable and he was good enough to comply. But the sang froid of the whole thing amused me. At home there would have been courts of inquiry and the Lord knows what. Later, I dined with Neil – and drank Scotch.

The first day at Ben Gardane was too busy to rate as a day at all, but 3 March started out a perfect pearl of a morning. First it was really good to be alive. Then there was the sea which, as the day progressed, became absurdly blue. The breezes were softly caressing and there was never a fly. John Richardson succeeded in finding some horses. After lunch, he and Neil and I drove into HQ of the French gendarmerie to find three horses saddled and bridled and ready for us, each held by a groom. Just as we had mounted, we were stunned to see two French officers drive in with a very presentable blonde seated between them. Were our splendid allies ever without the fair sex? There had even been a woman in the Teilim Hills – the driver of the French general's staff car. It was four months since any of us had even seen an elderly Arab woman in the far distance, let alone a European close to, and a pretty one at that.

However, we rode out for a couple of hours, 'away from it all'. It was even better than a swim in that respect. I had not felt so remote from war since Beirut. Once we came in sight of the road and could see tank-transporters and guns moving up, but 'Nothing to do with us,' we said. 'Come on, let's have a race!' I was on quite a nice little grey, but Neil's snaky little bay turned out to be 'the bullet' of the party and streaked away up the sandy track through the palm-grove, the shallow, dry sand making for good going. We must be forgiven for galloping a bit more often than we would have on other days. At least we brought them in dry and that night slept like logs for nine uninterrupted hours.

In spite of office work and two telephones that never kept quiet for an instant, I tried to make a point of riding every afternoon or evening. But even I could not keep it up. There was just too much to attend to if we were to get back into the line in little over a fortnight's time. For example, we were riding home one afternoon when a jeep came towards us in a hurry. The driver told us of a suddenly convened squadron leaders' conference. We left John to ride and lead while the jeep driver got onto the other horse. Neil and I sped back in his vehicle. The reason for this untimely conference? The arrival in the area of the general [Horrocks] who had taken such a very violent dislike to the regiment back at Tmimi. He had marked his arrival by at once decreeing an 'Exercise for Local Defence'. Our own was pretty good, but he meant for the defence of Ben Gardane. This could hardly be expected to be received kindly. But, in all fairness, he would have looked, if possible, even sillier in our eyes if a German counter-attack (expected soon where we had just come from) had succeeded and caught him on the hop. As it happened, the model defensive battle for Medenine is, of course, famous, and the figure given us that evening for enemy tanks destroyed was fifty one.

It was a rainy night and pitch black until the Luftwaffe began dropping flares. But though we were unmolested, I never did get used to lying in bed listening to the ever-increasing roar of an enemy bomber homing in, as it seemed, on my bed. Even so, on 7 March, in spite of the fact that the enemy was withdrawing, we had to go out on the aforementioned exercise with two battalions of infantry. Ours not to reason why. But by 1943 people had learned to reason why, even, occasionally, to make reply. 'You are not paid to think' had long become old hat as a military comment. From a purely selfish point of view, this exercise meant that, as well as spending all day in the orderly room (the new Daimlers and one hundred reinforcements had just arrived), I had to spend the whole night there as well compared with getting everything done by 6 p.m. then getting onto a horse for an hour or two. I was not alone in sighing for General Herbert of precious memory.

There were more enemy aircraft overhead and the sky was dotted with black airburst as I crossed to the mess on 8 March for lunch. It was Colonel George's thirty-sixty birthday. Inside, Judy Garland was singing on the wireless 'Mister Murray Taught Me Dancing in a Hurry!' Back in the office telephones rang, typewriters tapped, there were dreadful missives which needed really careful examination – war establishments and strength states – and everyone who passed by 'wanted a word with the adjutant'. Then 'A' Squadron returned with the first-hand accounts of the events at Medenine, making everything seem worth while again.

Peter told us that the Germans had evidently not expected to meet such resistance at first, their air recce having evidently shown them very little. They had therefore come swanning along, sitting up on their turret-tops 'as if they were going down the Wilhelmstrasse' until they met our dummy minefield, when they turned along its western edge and – 'Wallop! Lovely broadsides!' Their infantry then 'had a go', but had to fall back into some of the deeper wadis, which our Gunners had expected they would use, and had the range. Immediately they put down 'a wonderful concentration'. That same night a patrol of the Scots Guards got into a wadi and found enemy tanks and infantry forming up to attack 131 Brigade. This patrol got a message back, resulting in our Gunners 'letting fly with everything they had', pasting the place. When they let up, a German shouted an order and 'those few who could still obey skedaddled away roughly north west'. The Scots Guards patrol then went home, but when morning came at least one of the Scots had his 6-pounder inside an Italian hut. He let the German Mark IVs pass before 'shooting them up the backside, where they kept their engines'. Several tanks were destroyed in this way by what must have been exceptionally cool and brave members of the Brigade.

A Pole, who came across to us with his hands up, said that the Germans had been constantly on the go from one Tunisian front to the other. He had tried once to give himself up to the Americans, but failed to catch them up. We also heard that the Army Commander had described the latest engagement as the best example of a one-day battle, a triumph for the Gunners and Foot, and had already called it the Battle of Medenine. Morale was higher than ever when, that evening, George and I dined with Ned's 'C' Squadron. But I was not at my best state to receive the news next morning that we must have one squadron ready for the 15th, (four days' time) and the rest by the 17th, four days earlier than originally expected. I noted a little testily in my diary: 'The 11th Hussars were given from 25 January until yesterday and went 100 miles further back than us, to Bianchi.' All the same we were pretty well ready to go and we were cheered by a message to George from GOC 7th Armoured Division (General Erskine) thanking 12th Lancers 'for all you have done with the Division during the last two months. It has been very hard work for your Regiment, but they have been quite magnificent. We have always been so excellently served with information that I never had a moment's anxiety. Thank you very much.'

We were inoculated for TAB and that night I dreamed I was a train, then that I was a passenger and if I got out at the next station the pain would cease. Then that I had shaved with a blunt razor and was so thirsty I had drunk my soapy shaving water. But I felt perfectly well in the morning except for a very stiff arm, which was just as well as there were a host of last moment matters to be cleared. But things went well mainly, if not wholly, thanks to Sergeant Ingram. As usual.

Michael de Piro left me to return to 'B' Squadron as a troop leader. I missed his help and I missed him in the mess. His was an eye to catch. He was of the greatest assistance, too, with the 'callers in' who bedevil headquarters messes when they are temporarily beyond shot or shell. Just before lunch was a dangerous time. That or 6 p.m.

A group of our own officers and a couple of gin-and-tonic-seekers from elsewhere were seated in the sun outside the mess just before luncheon when twelve Baltimores flew over, having just taken off from the nearby landing ground. I had not seen them before and remarked on the fact, adding, rather obviously, that they made an encouraging spectacle.

'They're Bostons,' said one of the visitors.

I was in no way air-minded but fear had made my aircraft recognition unquestionable over the past three and a half years.

'Baltimores,' I murmured.

'Bostons', he said, noticeably piqued. 'Bet you a tenner!'

'Make it a pony,' I said.

I sent for Sergeant Ingram. As the RAF was geographically so close to us, he was able to go across to them straight away. He was soon back again with a sheet of paper, stamped by them and bearing the signatures of half-a-dozen RAF officers, on which was written in capital letters: ONE HUNDRED PER CENT BALTIMORES! Ingram had acted swiftly and with his customary thoroughness, but I never saw my pony.

Being so near the RAF, our telephone conversations could get mixed and we sometimes heard our neighbours loud and clear. For example, seventeen Baltimores took off one day and about forty minutes later returned mercifully 'all on'. A bit later I was interested to overhear, while waiting on the line to Tripoli, a rather nasal voice report: 'Trouble-free, no fighter, no flak, and every pilot is confident the bombs were square on target.'

A sharp authoritative voice rapped back that this was the 'SASO from Advanced HQ' and that the bombs had fallen 'eight miles off course on the 51st Highland Division'.

'Oh,' breathed the nasal one.

'Yes! So come up here *yourself* – NOW! Do you understand?' In view of the recent exercise, it was a wonderful relief to come under command of 1st Armoured Division again on return to the Medenine area. It was nothing less than marvellous to leave Horrocks's command, especially having spent so much time on the telephone to Tripoli that on one occasion I asked for Tripoli instead of the salt at luncheon. We set off for Medenine on 18 March at 7.30 a.m. in glorious weather, meeting the Army Commander, who leaned forward in the back of his open staff car, saluting and looking up at each turret as we passed. George was to dine with him that night. Much as I had loved the riding, Ben Gardane had lost its charm. Now I felt as if we were going home. We stopped at a small oasis from which ran a wadi with green strips of barley and vegetable patches with carrots once more to relieve the monotony of our nightly stew. We heard that the Americans had retaken Gafsa, the enemy having brought troops from that front in order to be strong before Medenine. We were also given the appalling tidings that 201 Guards Brigade had lost twenty-seven officers and hundreds of Guardsmen on the night of the 16th. This was later confirmed as twenty-four officers and 300 men of 6 Battalion, Grenadier Guards.

On the morning of 20 March I overheard on the R/T Desmond Fitzpatrick, our G1 of division, saying to somebody: 'Did you know that Scruffy has got a DSO?' So later on, when I saw my commanding officer, I said: 'May I congratulate you on winning the DSO, Colonel?' 'How the devil did you know?' he replied. It was a compliment to the regiment really, he modestly explained, and went once again to dine with General Montgomery to celebrate.

On the night of the 21st we gathered around the wireless set to listen to Winston Churchill, now back in London. Soon after first light we met Peter Gregson again. He had kept a bitch he had found in Zouara and I remembered my dear friend in El Assa. His bitch, he said, had already had puppies. 'Like little balls of fur they are, sir!' cut in his sergeant, bursting with enthusiasm. This unwarlike conversation took place on a visit to 1 Armoured Division and 22nd Armoured Brigade, shortly after which I was smothered in dirt by a bomb dropped on us by another 109. All dirt, no hurt, but the rather depressing news was that the Germans, having retaken some of our infantry positions, were holding up the New Zealanders (directed on Gabes) with their artillery. This sort of thing just would not do for the Army Commander and a conference was at once called at Divisional HQ, which George and I attended. Dick Taylor, a familiar Northumbrian landmark, was one of a host of racing men I immediately recognised even if I did not know them personally – and 'all with smiling faces'. The plan given us was the now famous 'Left Hook'. 1st Armoured Division was to move round the southern flank of the Mareth Line to join the New Zealanders forthwith. Although the dashing back to our various units with the urgent news was exciting, the whole business of getting our detailed orders to squadrons in the minuscule time available was less so. But all, of course, was made ready. Away we went as a regiment on the dot of 7 p.m. We went through Medenine and, coming to Foum Tatouhine in white moonlight, I got a charming impression of cottages and elms on one side, the edge of the forest on the other. In reality, shacks and eucalyptus trees on the one hand, palm groves on the other, but how imagination can improve the hour!

We emerged into the open and continued south at an increased pace. It was all highly enjoyable. The responsibility of map-reading temporarily belonged to some one else as we drove fast through the moonlit night. Only when we turned off the road into the desert, did we have to slow considerably as we came to the gap in the hills found by the Long Range Desert Group. Having passed through that, we followed the New Zealanders' tracks till 4 a.m. We had covered ninety-six miles, non-stop, after which we were allowed one hour's sleep, fully dressed, before completing the extra forty-two miles which took us right through the New Zealanders. 'At 18.25 hours', says my diary, 'we arrived eleven miles north of the enemy minefield, having passed through that as well.'

On 25 March we moved forwards in a following wind, invisible in a thick fog of dust that had more substance than smoke. Everyone either looked like a busy miller or a snowman. Friends were unrecognisable. We had been ordered to point 9990, and George had sent me ahead to meet the representatives of the other regiments there. These were Stug Perry (9th Lancers), George Streeter (Bays) and Douglas Kaye (10th Hussars). Luckily for everybody, these officers had at once discerned that point 9990 was held by the Germans. They had therefore already allotted assembly areas, including one for Divisional HQ before a slightly harassed major from there, wearing a hat reminiscent of the French artist of pre-war fancy dress parties, arrived late with an unwieldy and elaborately-marked map to tell everyone where to go.

'Well, no,' said Major Perry, calmly matter-of-fact as he studied the newcomer's map. 'We're already there. And, incidentally, your approach routes are impassable for vehicles and your assembly areas are the enemy FDLs.' Jack Price then arrived on the dot with his squadron of 9th Lancers.

We had already passed lorryload after lorryload of Italians, part of the 2,000 prisoners from their Pistoia Division, including one hugely fat officer, covered in medals, with a great black beard and flowing whiskers. He was experiencing grave difficulty in maintaining his dignity while having to sit up on the roof of a truck's cab which was bumping and swaying most cruelly through the deepening ruts of a very dusty track. George turned right round to watch him for quite a long time. He was suffering from an aching neck and shoulders, a legacy from Sandown Park where he had once broken his neck riding a horse called The Ace. 'He hasn't fallen off yet,' he said, 'but he will. Seeing him has made my day!'

A *khamsin* began to moan over the scorched wastes, sapping our energy as we prepared for the attack which was to go in at 4 p.m. I climbed up on to the turret half an hour before the 'off' and sat there waiting for Neil. We watched 7 Motor Brigade moving up in a choking white dust which was beginning to contain locusts the size of pea-pods, wafting into the cars on the hot, strong wind. Yet despite the thousands of vehicles and the dense fog of dust, each unit found its correct route (through the next minefield) and got itself tucked up into the queues in the correct order. That there were positively no mistakes at all under such conditions was, to me, just a triumph of organisation, discipline and experience.

After the RAF had spread a blanket of bombs in front of the New Zealanders, their attack went in. When the RAF and the infantry had done their stuff, we were to go through and push straight for El Hamma, leaving the Matmata Hills in the Mareth Line to our right, thereby threatening the latter with being cut off. Ned's 'C' Squadron was leading the way with 2 Armoured Brigade. 'A' and 'B' Squadrons were acting as flank guards to the artillery. So we now had Friz Fowler, Len Livingstone-Learmonth and Dick Taylor with us for direct and instant artillery liaison. We kept on the move all night, 88s still firing from close in front, their shells passing harmlessly away over our heads. We met hordes of prisoners newly taken by the New Zealanders, their white German caps bobbing silently along in the dark toward our rear. Most carried bundles, some were on stretchers and each party was escorted through the night by just two infantrymen. 'C' Squadron and the 9th Lancers were doing great things so that glowing 'cigar-ends' began to dot the darkness ahead. One of these turned out to be no less than three 88s all together in a blazing group. Their ammunition was exploding in a crackling inferno which painted the sky, desert and the passing British columns a rosy red.

So came yet another grey wartime dawn. As it came, Rod, protecting our right rear as we proceeded northwards, reported enemy tanks debouching from the hill, heading after us and engaging our tail. We were able to pass this information to Friz Fowler within seconds.

Everything went like a dream. The drill which followed might have been carefully rehearsed for a demonstration on Laffan's Plain. It was a pleasure to see at the time as well as to remember in the safety of retrospect. Our 'A' and 'B' Squadrons swung outwards to the flanks before facing about and engaging the tanks with their 2-pounders. The anti-tank gunners also swung outwards and about-turned, taking up a position astride the track we were using, facing south. The RHA came through and proceeded to shoot both ways, while the 10th Hussars (in reserve with 2nd Armoured Brigade, which was leading our advance) turned round and came racing back through us all, a fine sight, to engage the enemy tanks in front of our anti-tank Gun screen. Meanwhile the 8th Armoured Brigade to the east was closing on the tails of these enemy tanks. Rod won the MC for alerting us.

That having been satisfactorily dealt with, 'C' Squadron, in front, now reported the enemy 'swanning madly between El Hamma and Gabes'. The enemy left in the Mareth Line must have been getting nervous. We ourselves were virtually surrounded six miles south of Hamma, but we were advancing, palpably winning and, as one might say, consolidating our gains. At least we were sure we were not going back this time. When we moved on next day I rode with George and General Freyberg, while 'A' Squadron looked for a route which would take the latter's New Zealanders round the enemy flank. The enemy was still in Hamma and Rowly Beech 'took prisoner a hundred or so Wops in the hills'. I thought they resembled an infantry attack in strength and Stukas arrived with a lot of 109s to bomb both them and us. Our own anti-aircraft fire was more dangerous than they were, for there were bits and pieces humming and singing all over the place. However, there were no casualties.

A lot of enemy shelling in the evening continued long after dark. But it was indeed 'shot-in-the-dark' stuff and one felt it was the enemy's swan song as far as Hamma was concerned.

Indeed, 'C' Squadron went straight into the place at dawn and out the other side taking '100 plus prisoners and shooting up Itis north of there'. Reports came in from Alan Carson and a comparative newcomer, Tony Rankin, and from Sergeant Maguire (who had been leading a troop for a long time) describing the Italians as 'swarming in and out of holes like rabbits in a warren'. Nevertheless, we were heavily shelled in Hamma and there were casualties. To make sure of our left flank, 'A' Squadron went in the dark of night all the way to Kebili, fifty miles to the west. The Stukas were busy again and Michael Bradstock was wounded in the arm. We also heard that the Rifle Brigade had had many casualties which included fifteen officers. We had come to the impregnable-looking Wadi Akarit.

12

Forward to Tunis

On 31 March there was sporadic enemy shelling, but most of the shells went harmlessly over our heads to crash in open desert some distance behind. We counted quite a number of duds that failed to explode. That evening some mail caught us up. I received my Christmas cards – three months late.

On 1 April the very first report came, of course, from Tat. It was to the effect that there was 'an enormous battleship north of 6 Troop balancing on point 107 . . . ' This message was acknowledged without comment. After which the enemy started shelling again and Digby Thompson was hit in the head. The wound was said not to be serious, but Diggers was a serious loss to us. If Michael de Piro had been my right-hand man the previous August in the Alamein Line, Diggers had been my left. Luckily for us he managed to get back to the regiment before the campaign ended.

The following day, 2 April, was fairly static. The enemy had managed to extricate himself from the Mareth Line, although the 8th Army had taken a total of 6,000 prisoners in ten days. But he now seemed to be ensconced firmly enough in the Wadi Akarit. The Americans were loud and clear on our R/T sets, an almost constant source of amusement; their endless use of the word 'Roger' their equivalent of our 'O.K.', caused a smile or two, although we soon had to change to their system. 'Shells are boistin'all around!' we heard one of them shout, 'I'm gettin' the hell outa here!' 'Rarger!' cried the other.

I had to take myself away from this entertainment in order to seize the opportunity of taking one of the loveliest baths of my life. I was disgustingly grubby and determined to make use of Hamma's natural hot springs. A deep ditch, running with crystal clear water of the exact temperature which I would have chosen, served my needs. I had much the same feeling of well-being as I drove back to HQ as I had experienced after our swim in the sea on the eve of Alamein.

Leslie Monroe-Hinds had taken over from Michael de Piro. Older than me, he was one of the very few married officers. But I think he would agree that ours was as happy a partnership as could have been found throughout North Africa.

As night approached, enemy bombers started to wander about the sky and red tracer began to go snaking up into the royal blue of the late evening. All night these bombers dropped flares and it became a tiresome characteristic of the campaign from then on. One might just be falling asleep when their engines would begin to throb, nearer and nearer. Then the sound faded and with a sigh of relief, one would compose oneself again for slumber. But no. Here it came again, by the sound of things approaching in a nasty shallow dive, straight at you, personally. The sound of its engines was accompanied by a sort of whistling, slattering noise of a big aircraft flying very low – then: 'Wheeeeeeee! Ramp!', the first bomb – 'Worft!' the second and . . . ? Only two that time. And always those huge flares parachuting down so gently, lighting us up more clearly than a searchlight's beam. If we got all the sleep necessary, it was certainly disturbed.

We heard that Tony Wingfield (10th Hussars) had received four direct hits on his tank from 105s without being hurt. When some 109s came at me totally unexpectedly out of the afternoon sun, I was caught with my jeep, alone and right out in the open. Tony may have been lucky, but this time I would not be so. There was no time to do anything, but fall flat and pray. The ground erupted beneath me and I was flung against a wheel. Heavy stuff fell on my back and legs. I was deaf and choked. I lay there sniffing the familiar smell of cordite while dust and smoke began to clear. It was very quiet. I stood up. I was untouched and beat off the dust from my clothes, like beating a carpet, before picking up my hat and automatically looking to see if the cap-badge was still there. It was. The only damage was to the windscreen of the jeep, which was no more. I drove on into RHQ where Sergeant Charnell told me it was my turn for the bottle of whisky that occasionally came up with the rations. It could not have been better timed. Sergeant Charnell had grieved when one of his two hens, Sarah to be exact, had fallen from his lorry on the line of march. She had lost her balance and gone planing away down a long, steep slope to disappear for ever. She had laid 300 eggs and Sergeant Charnell had naturally found her loss hard to bear.

An attack went in at 4.15 a.m. on 6 April, which resulted in 2,000 prisoners being taken. By evening there were indications of the enemy pulling out and we moved east then north. There was a beautiful dawn on 7 April with larks rising from patches of wild flowers amid the shell holes. At 3.25 p.m. Tat shouted over the R/T 'Five is talking to Roger!' which meant that John Richardson's 5 troop had joined up with the Americans, an historic moment, the first contact of 8th Army with the US Army on the other front. He then shouted excitedly, 'We are just taking on some dug-in German lorries!' This message was followed by too long a silence and, when I tried to raise 'B' Squadron on the air, I eventually managed to get Matt, but not their HQ. He said: 'Neil and Tat have been put in the bag. Last seen going north in the back of an enemy lorry escorted by at least two tanks.' As we pushed on to the Fatnassa Gap, which gave the impression that it could have held till the end of time, we heard over the air that Dicky Hezlett and his troop had encountered this party of twenty lorries and engaged them. Neil had escaped, but they were still looking for Tat. In fact they had both baled out of their lorry and got clear, Tat turning up in due course. All was well that ended well.

We kept going forward all the next day, only once being attacked by 109s, one of which was 'hit in the beak' and fell more like a shot pheasant than anything else, turning a slow somersault as it plummeted down. Enemy tanks were in Mezzounia and a barrage of shells came creeping up the railway line towards my car with a steady and evil relentlessness. But it was in the nature of a parting shot, for it ceased abruptly and I could see enemy vehicles pulling out under cover of smoke. We with our two armoured cars spent the night with the 9th Lancers and, with a wall of tanks all round, I slept like the proverbial log.

I wrote in my diary that the next day was the most hectic in the war so far. It was not particularly dangerous. I must have meant that we maintained a fast pace all day long and in the right direction. I wrote that it was the nearest thing to foxhunting that you could get. We were all spread across the country. Now and then we came upon small wadis where there might be only two or three feasible crossings. On these we converged as might foxhunters at a gate or gap in an otherwise unjumpable fence. Sometimes there were too many queueing at the same place and one would pick somewhere else, get across and shove on, while the same people were still squashing at the original gap. We went through olive groves and across, I fear, some wide tracts of green, cultivated farmland. We began to pass isolated farm houses, white with red roofs and blue shutters, up hill and down dale.

After twenty miles of this headlong advance, twenty-two German tanks appeared some distance ahead but coming to meet us. The 10th Hussars came up from behind, went through us, set on fire two of them and sent the other twenty packing. They disappeared to the north as fast as they could lick. By that evening we were due west of Sfax and 8th Army had taken a further 9,000 prisoners since we left El Hamma.

On 10 April we found ourselves using good roads and the pace was corresponding. We crossed lush green countryside with patches of scarlet poppies, white daisies and pink clover. An Arab gave Booth two dozen eggs and thanked him for deliverance, but I think this must have been guided by the heat of the moment for, by and large, the Tunisian Arab liked us not. We picketed in a charming little olive grove at Chourbane. We had come there so fast that two formations of German heavy bombers passed over flying trustingly low, but just too far away for engaging. The pilots clearly imagined the area they were flying across was still German-held, having, in fact, only become airborne in the nick of time.

All things considered it was extraordinarily peaceful in that little green orchard. The sheep were making the same uproar as they do at home when rain is on the way. But the peace was quickly shattered after dark by the arrival of a strange truck and a loud and terrible half-hiss, half-shriek. I ran blindly out into the night to find that a Tank regiment driver had lost his way and driven right over the sleeping Sergeant Ingram. Onto him would be more accurate for, hearing the shriek, he had jammed on his brakes, pulling up with a wheel still on Ingram's chest. Rod and the others were soon on the spot and, with the driver, we all managed to lift the front of the vehicle high enough for Ingram to be extricated. I was fairly certain he would die, but Sergeant Ingram was tougher than he looked. He had gone to bed earlier in a shallow slit-trench where he knew no 12th Lancer vehicle would come anywhere near. I did not think that I had ever heard him swear. But now, when he was able to speak: 'Thank – Christ – it wasn't a ——g tank!' he gasped. I went to bed and dreamed of map references and by the grace of the Almighty, Ingram made a splendid recovery.

Next day I sat and copied our orders for an advance with a squadron of the Bays under command. The local Arabs got on with tilling the soil, their wooden ploughs being pulled by mixed teams of camels and mules. When I had finished writing, they had ploughed round me as if I were a tree. I would have moved if invited. Then George and I and RSM Harper had a canter round on a little bay horse, not *à la* Uncle Tom Cobley, but one at a time. It made Chourbane even more an oasis of peace.

By 5.30 a.m. we were on our way to Ksar, just south of Kairouan. We halted there and I dismounted in the hopes of having some breakfast. Instantly I was smothered in mosquitoes. It was as if they had grown on me. I was soon back on the turret beating at my clothes with both hands. Everyone seemed to be doing the same. To get, as the Americans had said, 'the hell outa there', was the only remedy. In fact, we covered a further fifty-four miles before we got our breakfast. 'A' squadron was busy taking prisoner some Panzer Grenadiers, but in so doing lost a scout car on a mine, killing Williams, the nicest of men, who had been Rod's driver for a long time. Sergeant Adams, MM, was wounded, the same 'Evie' Adams, as he was known, who had been in my troop in France and at Stuyvenskerke, just prior to La Panne and Dunkirk.

The regiment now went back under command of 1st Armoured Division and as we returned to Chourbane, we met the 11th Hussars moving up – Bill Wainman, Tony Crankshaw, Sandy Reid-Scott, Van Burdon, familiar faces all. The reason they were going forward and that we were going back was that we were to move by night to join 1st Army. I think the thing that most annoyed us was having to paint all our vehicles dark green, like those at home. Our vehicles were white, symbolic of the Desert Army. They had become a pinkish yellow and we were proud of this well-worn hue. Indeed it was a badge of honour for we had just advanced thousands of miles. We were also told to 'cut out the Arabic' which punctuated our every sentence. ('Maleesh' for 'What does it matter?' or 'Never mind', 'shufti' for 'look', 'yalla' for 'Go away' or 'Get out', 'talla hinna' for 'Come here'; etc., etc.,) Even though our Arabic was very far from extensive it was extensively used.

Some American soldiers arrived in a jeep, wanting to buy German souvenirs! Nutting, with a quick eye to business, immediately produced a Luger from nowhere. Taking it with shining eyes, one of our visitors proceeded without noticeable delay to shoot himself in the leg with it. Our ambulance had to be got into action and I saw to it that his friends accompanied it with their jeep, which got them all away for good. This was RHQ 12th Lancers, not the Portobello Road. Returning to my armoured car, however, I discovered a Rhode Island red roosting on the bonnet. On inquiry I was informed; 'She's the property of Mr Monroe-Hinds, sir. He had been shopping for the regiment in Sfax.' This information was vouchsafed by Trooper Norwood. Horace Norwood was a grocer from Leeds who had joined the regiment before we left England and, fortunately for me, became my servant at Khatatba. He looked after me to the manner born. It seemed the natural thing to do to call him by his Christian name. When I saw him about the place I felt relaxed. It usually meant I was having a better meal than usual, a bath, something pleasant. And I have always liked the phlegmatic men of Yorkshire. For example, on 17 April, I rose unhurriedly, shaved with hot water, then found my breakfast on a table with a chair for me to sit on. I breakfasted under an olive tree with the *Sporting Life* (three months old, but better than none at all) and spent a peaceful day in this shady grove, amidst its red and yellow blaze of wild flowers. All was ready. There was nothing more for me to do. And thanks to Mr Monroe-Hinds's recent purchase, my egg was a fresh one. At 6 p.m. that evening we got mounted and moved out. I occupied the command car in front.

As a regiment we raced along all through the night, reaching into Algeria. To get there we passed through acres of tented Americans (2nd US Corps) until we reached Sbeitla, the moon making more beautiful its ruins. It was a strange feeling passing these great pillars, still standing after thousands of years, and the moon-washed crumbling archways, thinking that here a civilisation once thrived. We turned north for Le Kef. As we were observing wireless silence, I asked Nutting if he could not raise some dance music. Presently, therefore, the music of Stan Atkins and his band stole into my earphones. Two tunes will always bring back those ancient moonlit ruins and the rush of the cool African night air – 'Murder, She Says', delivered by a splendidly strident young woman, and 'Kalamazoo'. We sped north, and to this light accompaniment I led the 12th Lancers under the stars into the dawn and a new green world, where the cuckoo took over from Stan Atkins. We had covered 180 miles and, instead of olive trees and palm, there were pines. We settled along the edges of a grassy valley as much like Six Mile Bottom as anywhere else I could think of.

Encouraging news came after breakfast that Sergeant Charnell had already managed to obtain some crates – crates, not bottles – of White Horse whisky (we had been too long on a rationed diet of an Australian brand), that cigarettes cost 30 francs less than with 8th Army and that the chocolate was Nestlé. Not perhaps news to stir the blood today, but my goodness it was then. George came in that evening, content with the general situation, having paid a visit to the 9th Lancers.

General Alexander came to see us on 20 April, an informal visit. True to the style of 8th Army he wore corduroy trousers and no medal ribbons on his shirt. Colonel George had for some time been wanting to get Sergeant Maguire commissioned, but this would have entailed this indispensable NCO having to go all the way back to the Nile Delta (still our base) and to go through an OCTU. He explained the problem to General Alexander, and the general asked me if I had a message pad. I handed him one. Leaning on the bonnet of my jeep, he wrote a message to General Jumbo Wilson informing him that he was making Sergeant Maguire an officer on the spot – or 'in the field', to be more correct. So Bob became an officer there and then, and I gave him a copy of the message in the general's own hand. I hope he was able to keep it. Bob fought the war with more élan than many, was always at the sharp end in order to push on (he had personally lifted mines recently by the light of a candle), and was eventually wounded and taken prisoner in Italy. In 1981 I met him at a luncheon (in his honour) in the officers' mess in Hyde Park Barracks, but forgot to ask him about the general's message of nearly forty years before.

After General Alexander came the divisional commander accompanied by Toby Whetherley and I conducted him through the regimental area. Armoured cars and other vehicles seemed to stretch for miles and I noticed several of the soldiers hacking about the valley on ponies. 'What a lot of people there are in a regiment!' I commented in my diary. It took quite a time to get all round. Having ridden on the leading car throughout the previous night, I was thankful to be able to go to bed early.

I had been asleep for half an hour when I was woken with the tidings that an order had just come in and the colonel wanted me to go over to his lorry and 'sort it out'. Squinting with sleep I got into my clothes. It was dark, raining hard and at least a quarter of a mile's walk to George's lorry. I arrived fairly wet to find my commanding officer having a night cap. 'Oh, hullo, Tim', he greeted me, 'have a drink? I just wanted to tell you to get some sleep because, as you know, 'A' Squadron is moving out early and I would like you to be up to see them go.' Anyone who may have heard me returning to my car must have thought 'a frightful fiend was walking close behind'. I peeled off my wet clothes and, awake at last, got back into bed. I never did get to sleep!

One of the first things we had noticed on this front was the shakiness of aircraft recognition. The appearance of a lone Kittihawk was enough to send lorry-loads of ammunition skywards into thin air. The excuse given was that for the first weeks of the 1st Army's arrival 'every aircraft was a hostile one'. So it had seemed to us before Dunkirk and, indeed, much later than that. But there was not a man of ours who would not have have recognised an Allied aircraft, even if he might get the name wrong. Recognised it and, I dare say, cheered it as well.

At 9.15 p.m. on 21 April Rod blew a note on his silver hunting horn in the dark as the signal for the 12th Lancers to move out of the trees and bushes and form single file down the valley and onto the road. We had thirty-eight miles to go with no lights and in wireless silence – so I got Nutting to tune into Joe Loss. We reached our new area in the small hours and slept till dawn.

The enemy was holding fast to the Barka feature, so when it grew light we moved north to a point just south of Goubellat. It was not long before Robin Brockbank had charged and destroyed a German 75 (says my diary, but it was afterwards said to be a 50 mm – lethal enough either way). He came on it unexpectedly from growing crops. His driver, Procter, was killed and his operator wounded, the car careering onto the gun, overturning it and getting stuck on the top. Robin was taken prisoner and, as the Germans started flinging grenades about, found himself in a slit trench with some of his captors. But when one of them put down his tommy gun, Robin snatched it up, shot all three of the Germans with it and then ran into the standing crops with his wounded operator. His other car had been blown to pieces on a big mine, only the rear wheels were left. Corporal Parker and Troopers Dines and Pardow had been killed. Bob Maguire saw Robin, who was later evacuated with a piece of shrapnel in his leg, and picked up both him and his operator. Robin was awarded the MC for this.

On 24 April we pushed on due east of Goubellat. Two Spitfires, with their roundels clearly recognisable, their unique shape unmistakable, flew low and confidently over us. They received a full complement of flak from our British neighbours. In consequence British bullets were singing and whining through our HQ and smacking into bushes past our legs. Something had to be done and I sent an officer across. He came back grinning. 'All I've got is a flea in my ear!' he said. We then heard that the RAF had shot down twenty out of twenty six-engined German transports over the Gulf of Tunis. But if this sort of thing went on, there might soon be no RAF planes left either.

Our life was made easier by having Desmond FitzPatrick of the Royals and Toby Whetherly as G1 and G2 of Division. Common sense, broad-mindedness, and a sense of humour held sway. And my immediate associates were towers of strength. With George Kidston commanding, Rodney Palmer as second in command, Leslie Monroe-Hinds as assistant adjutant, Sergeant Ingram as my orderly room sergeant, and Horace Norwood to look after me in other ways, no one was better off. Furthermore, I had had Trooper Simmons driving my 'armoured' for some time after Booth was promoted. He was a tough regular with a Cockney sense of fun and I had been touched, not to say moved, when on Christmas Day he and Nutting had presented me with a new Ever Ready razor in the 'middle of nowhere'.

The night of the 24th was as dark as the inside of a cow. First, George had to go off into the blackness to get fresh orders, then Neil had to move his squadron at 1 a.m. along difficult tracks not marked on any map. Like his shadowing of the enemy's advance through the minefields in a dense sandstorm before Alam Halfa, by getting his squadron to the right place at the right time in the dark, he again demonstrated his ability to achieve the impossible with an airy unconcern. I was up throughout the night, first alerting Neil's squadron who had turned in, not expecting to be disturbed, then getting orders to Ned's squadron and trying to find the right people in a darkness so pitchy that it had the unusual characteristic of remaining dead black however long you were out in it. At a quarter to five in the morning we moved RHQ as well, going with the divisional commander nearly to the Kournine feature, a twin-peaked hill rather like a Durham slag-heap covered in grass. But at least we could see where we were going.

Here the 17th/21st Lancers and the 16th/5th Lancers were being pretty accurately shelled and the 9th Lancers, 10th Hussars and Queen's Bays were waiting to follow up any success. It looked like a lot of tanks out in the open, spaced stationary across the flat ground to the south-west of Kournine. But the ground favoured the enemy who was out of sight in broken ground north of the feature, and he had plenty of guns in his perimeter. During the morning Trooper Ryan, of whom Neil thought a lot and of whom he was fond, was killed beside him. Then came the final straw.

A lone Hurricane, flying perhaps at less than 1,000 feet, flew back from the direction of the enemy and straight as a die south over the 1st Army sector. At once a curtain of British flak rose about it. Not unnaturally its pilot began to take evading action, waggling his wings, which was, as well, a signal of friendship. If anything it increased the volume of fire. Those who shot at it, and they were legion, must have been excruciatingly bad shots for on and on the poor devil flew through their hail of lead. We yelled at them, gesticulated, danced up and down, but what was the use in such a crescendo? Because the guns in front were firing at the plane, those further back took it up. The Hurricane dived perpendicularly into the ground and exploded. A lot of British soldiers emerged from slit trenches (whence they had gone for protection from one of their own aircraft) cheering and, believe it or not, *clapping*. We cursed them, but they were pale-faced and cursed us back with a small-eyed and nervous fervour.

All this time there was very considerable air activity, but at the time of that solitary Hurricane's passing, it had been the only plane in the whole sky. But that night we were bombed by German bombers and so was the echelon. Bill Mabbott's driver, Wilkinson, was killed. Next morning Junkers 88s and Heinkels came over, hotly pursued and being engaged by Spitfires. I was watching a Spitfire closing on the tail of a Heinkel when the Spitfire vanished. Just one wing-tip came spiralling down like a leaf. Throughout, the ground troops kept up their fire at the planes – at the Germans, yes, but the attacking Spitfires were virtually of the same formation. In our book, bombers that were being taken on by our own fighters were not engaged.

General Dick McCreery paid us another informal visit. He said everything was going well, the Rifle Brigade was to attack that night and that he was going over to 8th Army next day 'to ginger up Monty as we expect more help from that quarter'. I then seized the opportunity of reporting the trigger-happiness affecting Allied aircraft and he agreed it was 'very bad' and told me to report further instances 'in detail if possible'.

Easter Monday and a message came in which I thought worth recording for posterity if only to give an example of red tape. We were, at the time of its arrival, at the receiving end of some heavy shelling and the Hermann Goering Regiment in front was showing no signs of giving up. Their only visible reaction to being sprayed with machine-gun fire was the more frequent appearance of their pickaxes above the earth's surface as they more firmly dug themselves in. This message, under the circumstances, was a classic of its kind. It read: 'From G.E.O. Mid East AF/38193.7915049 L/Cpl (so-and-so) to report Education Office HQ BTE opposite Egyptian Museum, KASR EL NIL. CAIRO at 1030 hrs 26 April' – which date it was anyway and Cairo was 2,000 miles away. A little light relief never went amiss. We were bombed again during the night with butterfly bombs and several vehicles were set on fire. The Rifle Brigade's attack was held up by MKIV tanks with 88s mounted on them. Three of their carriers were brewed up and the supporting arms failed to get up over the bad going.

Two of John Richardson's cars received direct hits with high explosive. No one was killed, but there were hospital cases. John was again untouched. Matt added to his now considerable list of exploits by climbing to the summit of Kournine and finding four sleeping Germans on the top. One of these he shot dead with his revolver when he attempted to retaliate. As he was bringing the other three down, one of them threw a grenade and Matt had to get out quickly.

Just after this George and I visited 'B' Squadron troops and, as at Himeimat, our arrival coincided with that of a number of shells from the opposition. Again George was dismounted and this time fell. He had been struck in the back of the knees, either by stones or blast. It looked bad, but he was unscathed. Then some Hurricanes came over and were heavily engaged on sight by our British neighbours. It was a simple matter to note which groups had fired and, having pinpointed them, I sent all available officers to find out who they were. Five days later I wrote in my diary: 'Success. Reporting the trigger-happy has resulted in an order being issued to all A/A Batteries. During the past three days we have all noticed a remarkable change. Now they only shoot at the enemy.' It was by no means the anti-aircraft batteries, only a few of which were the culprits, but the order had circulated far and wide and all the signs showed that it had struck home in the right quarters.

The enemy stayed where he was regardless and we sat on in the green cornfields constantly sending back information. An example was: 'Those six 75s are still behind the Argoub feature. Their shells are falling at 782204. Machine-gun fire from point 203 and 2 tanks have moved west into hull-down positions in bushes at 796224 or 5.' After a pause of a minute: 'Three 88s are shelling the areas south west of Kournine. Probably two 105s as well, but I will confirm that. Heavy shelling now.' So it went on without cease.

1 May the Bays successfully shot up some enemy infantry. Our 'B' Squadron came into reserve and the place became quite social in a different way from the dread social round at home. Neil, Matt, John Richardson and

Michael de Piro all called in and I never saw more cheerful people. Their exuberance was a tonic. Ian Walker and two other Derbyshire Yeomen called and Mick Lindsay, too, about the KDGs taking over. Not an enemy plane did we see all day and things became quiet on the ground as well.

It was the same next day, a Sunday. Just the twittering of larks going up and up into the sky and only very occasionally the far distant thump of an explosion. Monday was the same. It was rather uncanny, though we did hear that the Americans had taken Mateur just south of Bizerta, which 'must have been disquieting for the foe'. It almost seemed as if everybody had realised it was silly to go on and the war was petering out of its own accord.

On 4 May George suggested I take advantage of the lull to 'go and see my friends'. I went in search of the 17th/21st and found Mike Watson and George Brooke. We lay in the sun on a grassy bank and exchanged news.

5 May was still quiet. I passed it reading *Horse and Hound* (only five weeks old) until late when Neil and Ned joined Leslie and me for as merry an evening as anyone could invent. But the next day started with the spectacle of no less than fifty of our bombers escorted by at least as many of our fighters roaring steadily towards Tunis unopposed. The swing of the pendulum. Again, in the afternoon, I counted a hundred bombers with fifty fighters flying north. Not a gun was fired.

But the quiet of the past few days was breaking. That morning Rowly Beech's car was hit by a well-concealed 50mm, a second car going up on a mine. Dismounted, his troop was machine-gunned and mortared, but retaliated with grenades and managed to extricate itself in dribs and drabs on foot without casualties. RHQ was accurately shelled in the afternoon, but this attack through Medjez straight for Tunis was continuing and we learned that the 11th Hussars had now, like ourselves, been brought round to this front, 'which', comments my diary, 'automatically ensures them the best draw on the stands side for being first into Tunis'.

At last on 7 May the enemy in front of us appeared to be withdrawing. The attack in the north was going well, which would partly account for this. 'B' Squadron took 200 German prisoners and Dicky Hezlett captured single-handed a German company. There began a general move forward past Kournine. I looked up at this hill and wondered not only at the guts but at the agility of Matt, that he should reach the top accompanied by only one other and armed with just a revolver. He had not known what he would encounter and his climb had been to find out just that.

Tunis was in Allied hands by 4 p.m. So was Bizerta. But we were still sitting on mudflats in a cold, pelting downpour while our Gunners shelled the enemy over our heads. Orders for the following day came in at midnight. From then until dawn, therefore, in an unforgettable night of incomparable wet and blackness, I stumbled round knee-deep crops between George's lorry, the orderly room truck and the regimental forward link. But worse was to come. The orders had to be got to 'B' and 'C' Squadrons. Again there was no light showing anywhere to guide me. The crops wrapped themselves about my knees while a rising half-gale slashed rain into my face. I felt that the rain must be of the Germans' making. It had saved their bacon immediately after our breakthrough at Alamein and was making life ten times more difficult now. It would have been extremely difficult to find the right places with a strong torch. I was as wet as if I had been swimming under water; there was laughter when I reached my two goals. Getting back to my own car was just as difficult.

As dawn broke, George Rich (a lifelong friend, in the Queen's Bays) went by in a truck with a dog sitting beside him. Suddenly it went into a skid in the mud and turned upside down. Sergeant Major Knight, a man who only had to raise one finger for chaos to become order, got the thing righted, picked up George and his dog and set him on his way. George said he was sorry he could not stay for breakfast. He gave me the impression of one who overturns his truck every day for fun.

A certain member of the Royal Signals owed his life to Sergeant Major Knight. As no 12th Lancer was available, a Signalman once took me across to Divisional HQ. When we got there I saw him light a cigarette. I told him to put it out at once and went into the HQ tent. Then I heard the bump of a minor explosion and ran back outside. The Signalman was a pillar of flame. Disobeying my order, he had opened his truck bonnet to do something to the carburetter with the cigarette still between his lips. It had blown back. Sergeant Major Knight happened to be close by, dived for the man's bedding on the truck and, with the blankets spread out, just leaped on top of him. It quenched the flames at once. Although the man was badly burned, he owed his life to the Sergeant Major's quick thinking and action.

The rain stopped and for just two minutes I was able to watch in peace the flight of a large flock of flamingos. They flew about us changing direction from time to time, all simultaneously as by word of command. Now the flock was pink, now black and white, now pink again. It was a sight for the Gods.

But now prisoners of the Hermann Goering Regiment were beginning to come in. Once more, from the sublime to the ridiculous. We only moved on a short way, but 'C' Squadron was able to push south of Hammam Lif reporting enemy tanks. Studying the map as I marked their positions, I wondered if it was to be a case of pursuing them to the beaches as they had had to do with us at Dunkirk.

Sunday, 9 May started with a quick dash through a gap in some high hills. The order was to 'go fast and keep going' as the gap was still under shellfire. It was a case of running the gauntlet. But as we raced through, no gun was even heard and we reached without trouble a little village of red-roofed houses and green hedges called Khedia. Now the 10th Panzar Division surrendered and 30,000 enemy troops capitulated. What staggering news this would have been a few months before! But still in front of us was the 90th Light Division, old and respected acquaintances, fighting on. While 600 Hermann Goering Grenadiers 'made proposals to disarm and march west in threes with a white flag at their head', 300 Italians, hiding in a mine, refused to come out unless we stopped shooting. They surrendered that evening to Sergeant Cruden of 'C' Squadron, many of them in tears. Later on we were told 'not to molest' any enemy marching west in threes, even if they had no white flag. This was an example of the degree of their collapse. I got some sleep that night.

Leslie found and purchased some local wine from a warehouse in Khedia. But it was not just the wine – which had a kick almost comparable to whisky – that gave me a growing feeling of exhilaration and excitement. There were things like rose gardens, orchards, peaches, green trees, dusty lanes between hedges and the incredible prospect of actuallly finishing this long-drawn-out campaign for good, and victoriously.

'Three years ago today', I wrote on 10 May, 'we were going through Belgium to meet the Germans for the first time.' On 11 May we moved on again through the pass to Grombalia at the western end of the Cap Bon peninsula, in which all the remaining enemy was trapped. We passed destroyed 88s, 50mm anti-tank guns, wrecked tanks, burned out transport; everywhere was littered with abandoned German equipment. We sent lorry-loads of well-fed, surly looking youths of grand physique back to the prisoner of war cages in the rear-proper desperadoes, yet having the unmistakably attractive atmosphere about them of good soldiers. We moved into an extensive olive grove at Grombalia, dismounted with sighs of relief – and immediately came under the most concentrated shellfire. It transpired later that it was the work of three 88s getting rid of their last hundred rounds. It was a pity they had to choose our grove as their target.

George was near enough to the car to do a swan dive back into the turret. I was too far away to chance it and fell flat on my face. Shells were literally cascading about us, bursting in the branches as well as on the ground. It continued for what seemed a very long time – as long presumably as it took three 88s to get off one hundred rounds as fast as they could – and I thought, as I prayed with my nose in the grass, how typical of life to end at the very moment of final victory. Suddenly silence fell with surprising abruptness. I stood up, as did others all round me and men dropped down from their turrets to the grass. Not one man had been touched. That this should be so was a most incredible fact. The only casualty was Potter Miller-Mundy's 'armoured', destroyed by a direct hit. But, like me, he had been on the ground and he was only bewailing the loss of a bottle of whisky, more important, he said, than the lone survivor, a bottle of hair oil from Trumper's.

In case the Germans were only having a breather, we immediately moved under cover 300 yards to the other side of the road. But it had been their grand finale and I, personally, was never again shot at or bombed in Africa. We took Nabeul, cutting off the 90th Light Division from the peninsula – and I saw the sea again.

By this time there were German soldiers driving lorries and buses unescorted, picking up parties of their own troops for transporting to prisoner of war camps. It was a weird sensation to meet half-a-dozen lorries round a corner, crammed with Germans, only to pass without so much as a glance from them. As the afternoon went by, more and more such vehicles, packed to capacity, went along the Tunis road to the prisoner of war cages, none escorted. Some convoys were led by German officers riding in Volkswagens.

I took my evening meal in comfort beneath a large tree, tired but very happy. It might have been Hampshire with a final set of tennis in progress beyond the bushes. But it was nothing at all like tennis that was being played out to a finish. Michael de Piro took prisoner the G1 of 21st Panzer Division, who was so cross he deliberately knocked over our regimental sign beside the road when being brought in, like a naughty little boy being taken home early from a party. 'A' and 'C' Squadrons directed to the rear long columns of Germans in the area of Soliman.

The next day, 12 May 1943, was one of the most fascinating of my life. This was contrast with a capital 'C'. I woke early from a deep and uninterrupted sleep. There was not a sound. No rumbling of gunfire nor roar of aircraft. I cannot remember even one bird singing. I got up and washed and shaved without the telephone ringing or the wireless crackling out a message and breakfast was ready under the large tree when I was dressed. After which Leslie and I went to see what was going on in our immediate vicinity.

The thing I best remember was the arrival of two companies of German infantry from 90 Light marching smartly in, fully armed and under command of their officers. They halted beside us with a crash of boots, turned left and received the order to ground arms. Each man then took his pay book from his breast pocket for checking. They were on parade. They did not look at us, but straight to their front. On the command 'Fall out' they unslung their equipment and sat obediently on the roadside grass to await the next order. It was impressive and rather sad. My main feeling was one of embarrassment. For some extraordinary reason I felt ashamed.

I suggested to Leslie that we take my jeep and go to Tunis to see what was happening there. We could not have timed things better, though it was luck that we arrived in the town centre just as loudspeakers were announcing that L'Armée Brittanique was victorious. Lord Montgomery later wrote: 'It is about 2,000 miles from Alamein to Tunis, and we had got to Tripoli in three months and to Tunis in six.' And here indeed we were. There was a roar of applause, bravos and clapping which died away as the 'Marseillaise' struck up. It is one of my favourite tunes, so the fact that it goes on for some time did not worry me. We saluted, standing beside our battered and sand-encrusted jeep, while the sunshine brightened the tree-lined boulevards and shone on the girls all round us. A marvellous feeling of joy and relief infused us all. When it was over, the crowd began to disperse, cheering, shaking hands, hugging each other, laughing, crying: I have not, more is the pity, seen such 'come hither' again.

We had to get back. On our return journey all the vehicles going the opposite way towards Tunis were German. The occupants did not look at us. As we finished lunch, George came in and, ignorant of the fact that we had already been there, said 'Why don't you two go and take a look at Tunis?' Leslie's eye caught mine as we thanked him. Then once more we gratefully took the road.

But it was over. All was changed. The sparkle was gone of that magical hour which immediately followed the public announcement of victory. Hundreds of other soldiers had flooded in, French, Americans by the score, Indians and a few British, mostly non-combatant. Many were noisily drunk on the pavements, for wine was being given away everywhere. There was good reason to celebrate. But the girls of the morning had gone to ground, there were none to be seen. None. It was anti-climax and suddenly dull. We went to the park where we found General Giraud addressing French troops. As soon as he had been driven away in a staff car there came from the loudspeakers, rigged up in the trees, not the announcements and orders that might have been expected, but Jean Sablon singing 'Boom! Why does my heart go boom?' All very French and thoroughly unmilitary. My heart had gone 'boom!' in the morning, but not any longer. We were more than ready to drive back to RHQ, 12th Royal Lancers. We were at dinner when the BBC informed us 'All organised resistance in North Africa has ceased.'

Epilogue

The end of a campaign is inevitably something of an anti-climax. Formations break up, familiar faces disappear, and the trivialities of military life once again loom large. Tim Bishop had another seven months in North Africa during which he was promoted to command his old 'A' Squadron, after his long stint as adjutant. Although there were agreeable distractions, both feminine and equine (the latter being provided by a regiment of Spahis who had retained their horses), he was none too well, suffering from recurrent jaundice and an old back injury.

In January 1944 he flew back to England to attend a course, but was down-graded medically, and after postings to Sandhurst and then the Inns of Court Regiment – in connection with armoured car training – rejoined the 12th Lancers at Colchester before eventually leaving them after the war, at Barnard Castle – where there was more than a little hunting!

By this time he had married Clayre Paton and they were to live happily on the Border, near St Boswells. They had one daughter, Susan, who married a regular soldier, Tom Attwood, and the three children of this union brought great happiness to their grandfather.

In the postwar years Tim became a noted judge of hunters, and also wrote attractively on sporting matters. But, as ever, he was over-diffident about his own artistic talents. He died in 1986, a sad loss to his family and friends.

Index